PEEKS at the PEAK

Around and about the Peak District and Derbyshire near Sheffield
By Ann Beedham

Chatsworth, one of the best known attractions in the Peak District

Contents

This book is an attempt to put together some of the places and tales of the area that embraces Sheffield, Derbyshire and the beautiful part of the country we know as the Peak District, with its much loved National Park.

It is not meant to be a scholarly and detailed history, as there are many people who are more knowledgeable and could do a far better job than me. Instead it is a fond dip into things that will hopefully tempt you out again to explore anew the fascinating aspects of the Peak.

There is so much history around us to absorb as we wander today's wonders of the countryside and villages. You may be having a lunch stop on a bank once used by a weary leadminer to rest briefly after a backbreaking days work, and before a long walk home. Or you may sit on a millstone, abandoned after toil by a long gone worker, who had sweated under the sky, too busy to enjoy the stunning views.

As well as industrial history, there are lovely churches and halls to see, where generations have worshipped, worked, sang, laughed, loved and grieved, and indeed still do.

And there are of course the natural wonders, which have impressed an endless stream of visitors to varying degrees over hundreds of years. So pack the flask and sandwiches and go and take a peek for yourself!.

This book is dedicated to my soulmate and husband Edward, who shares my love of history and the Peak District and with whom the journey through life's wonders is even more of a blessed and beautiful adventure

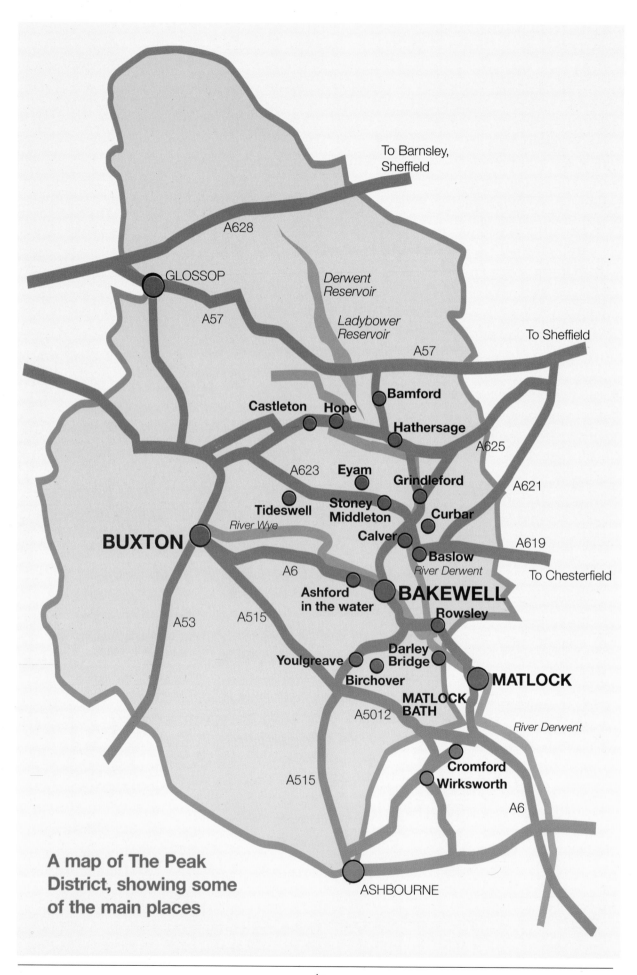

A map of The Peak District, showing some of the main places

The Peak District

The area known as The Peak has within it a National Park. This park was the first one created, in April 1951, and covers not just Derbyshire, but also areas of the counties of Staffordshire and Cheshire...

The Peak District is sometimes thought of as just the area that is covered by the National Park, but the park in fact excludes a lot of it. The district draws flocks of visitors from far and near to sample its many charms, which range from rivers to mines, from caverns to beautiful buildings and of course the stunning scenery.

A National Treasure

Though it is partly a National Park, the majority of the land in The Peak District is still privately owned, much by farmers. The National Trust and water companies also own a large part of it. Some of the areas are managed for grouse shooting. Access agreements, however, have meant people can still enjoy the places too, with footpaths and rights of way.

How did the Peak District get its name?

This subject is often debated. Some say the name 'Peak District' is a modern invention, from the 20th century, as tourism became more popular and the area more well known.

It is widely accepted that the name does not come from hills or peaks, of which there are none of great size, the largest probably being Win Hill, Mam Tor or Lose Hill. Instead it comes from an old English word peac, meaning hill or knoll, which was in the name given to the people who lived here in the 7th century AD - the Pecsaetna. or hill dwellers. So if people come expecting lots of pointed mountains they won't find them!

Archaeology

The area has long been home to various peoples. Many hills have burial mounds and there are also quite a lot of stone circles. Most impressive of these are Arbor Low, sometimes called the Stonehenge of the North, the Nine Ladies on Stanton Moor and the circles on Barbrook Moor.

Ancient routes

Throughout the Peak District are many old and new way marked paths and trails, from salt routes to old railway lines, now forming cycle routes. Old paths can still be seen, as hollow ways and tracks that still exist, or that have their lines now overlaid by modern roads for horseless carriages.

One of the oldest paths still to exist is The Portway. This and other paths would have been trodden in all weathers by the hardy packhorses and their human leaders, the jaggers. They would have wound their way with salt and other goods over the hills. Old pack horse bridges mark their routes, such as the one at Bakewell.

Millstones and lead, too, would have been transported along the routes now trodden by walkers.

Some medieval causeways, laid out with smooth stones wide enough for a single horse, and sometimes thought to be Roman, also exist in the Peak landscape. Best known is the one near Stanedge Pole.

Later came the turnpike roads, making travel and tourism easier and leaving us with reminders in the form of old toll houses, such a that at Stoney Middleton. The turnpike roads formed the basis for many of the modern roads which cross the Peak District today.

In the 19th century came the railways, and the associated tunnels, such as the Totley Tunnel which can be seen well at Grindleford, and the viaducts, such as the one at Monsal Head.

Industries

Running through the land are mineral veins, with lead ore and flourspar. This has led intensive mining in the area over the centuries and The Peak District has a wealth of industrial archaeology. The lead mines at Odin and Sheldon and caverns at Castleton are still a stark reminder of the hard won ore and give us a taste of the conditions of those mining for it, or for the famous gem Blue John.

Millstones for grinding grain and, later, cutlery, were hewed from the gritstone, giving the edges their characteristic shapes.

Peak traditions

Many old traditions still remain or have been revived in the Peak. Well dressing now flourishes again and has great tourist appeal. This custom is thought to originate from when wells and water were seen as a focus for offerings to the gods/goddesses.

The Castleton Garland is another ceremony that maybe has echoes of elements of ritual beheading or hanging.

PEAK DISTRICT
NATIONAL PARK

The White and the Dark Peak

The Peak District can be roughly divided into two areas, the White Peak and the Dark Peak. They both have different characteristics.

The Dark Peak

This area is higher and wilder. Gritstone and shale give the darker colour. The gritstone areas of the Peak have long been a major source of stone used for building and for millstones. Millstone production was one of the main industries of the area in medieval times.

Millstone Edge, above Hathersage, earns its name from this activity.

Many abandoned millstones can be seen still today, including a large pile of them at Bole Hill Quarry, near the Surprise View.

This quarry was also used to produce stone for the mighty dams of the Upper Derwent Valley.

Many of the edges once used for millstones are now the haunt of climbers, for whom the Peak District is a great attraction with many routes. Stanage Edge is one of the best known ones.

The Peak District is also sometimes divided into three 'character' areas, the White Peak, The Dark Peak and The South West Peak.

The White Peak

This is an area of carboniferous limestone. Parts of the Peak were once covered by a warm inland sea about 345 million years ago. Limestone is a sedimentary rock made of the remains of creatures and plants that lived in this sea, such as brachiopods, trilobites and crinoids (sea lilies). As these creatures died, the softer parts of their forms decomposed, leaving the harder shells or stalks to fall and settle on the sea bottom. Over millions of years, a layer of this debris built up and became compacted, eventually forming limestone. Fossils of some of these creatures, can often be seen in the resulting rocks.

Limestone has been used as a building stone for hundreds of years., for houses, barns and walls. It was also used for lime-burning. The limestone was burned in kilns. Lime was one of the main constituents of mortar for building and was also used on soil to reduce acidity.

Another use of lime was to make limewash, an early form of paint. This has been used in Britain since Roman times, to protect stone and buildings. It is a good method as it still allows the stone to 'breathe.' Limewash is becoming more popular again today as old buildings are restored using the original methods and materials.

Today limestone is used for many things, including crushed rock or aggregate for road making, and cement production.

Abandoned millstones at Bole Hill Quarry near Grindleford

Castleton

A view of Castleton from Peveril Castle

This picturesque village is one of the most popular places to visit in the Peak District. As well as the castle there are caverns where a rare gem, Blue John, is found

Castleton lies between the Dark and the White Peak, the gritstone and the limestone. The name 'Castle town' comes from the Norman Peveril Castle, whose keep has dominated the skyline for centuries.

An ancient settlement

At the edge of the village is a brooding hill known as Mam Tor, the shivering mountain. On top of here is the earliest known settlement of the village, an Iron Age hillfort, though people may have lived in the area since much earlier times than that.

The church

St. Edmund's Church. Right is the arch with Norman decoration

A wing faced cherub from a gravestone at the church

One of the names carved on the pews, with the date 1661

SAMUEL CRYER 1661

At the heart of the village of Castleton is the church of St. Edmund's. It is an atmospheric spot, with interesting graves surrounding it. Much of the present building dates from extensive renovations of 1837, though the tower dates from 1220-60. There are many other clues to its great age, including a Norman arch and a Saxon piscina in the wall inside. There are some fine 17th century pews too, with the names of the people who once sat there and the dates.

Also in the church are two old bibles, with special significance. The 'Vinegar Bible' was published by John Baskett in Oxford, England in 1717. It is called the Vinegar Bible because one of

The Vinegar Bible that can be seen in the church

The parable of the vinegar

S. Luke.

the headings in Luke 20 contained a misprint, reading 'Parable of the vinegar' instead of 'vineyard'.

The other bible is a 'Breeches bible' of 1611. This is so called because in Genesis 3 verse 7 it has "They sewed fig leves together and made themselves breeches." (instead of aprons)

Near the church is the pretty 17th century Castleton Hall, now a Youth Hostel

The war memorial in the square

Peveril Castle

The village of Castleton, as the name suggests, is dominated by Peveril Castle, once called the Castle of the Peake. The original Norman castle was built soon after the Norman conquest of 1066 by a man called William Peverel, a powerful man in the reign of William I, who was granted many manors, including that of Castleton. His high favour with the king gave rise to the belief that he was the bastard son of William the Conqueror.

The castle is in an enviable position for defending the land around, with the natural protection of sheer rock and steep slopes.

The castle we see today, most notably the keep, was built after the Peverel family left and dates from 1176, during the reign of King Henry II.

It was built to oversee the King's Royal Forest of the Peak. Little of the forest remains now.

For a short while the castle was in the hands of Simon de Montfort, until he was killed in battle, when it became crown property again.

The castle fell into disuse in the early 15th century and became a picturesque ruin. The keep has three floors, with access at the first floor. The facing stones from the outside have fallen or been taken over the years, leaving the rubble core exposed.

The castle is now looked after by English Heritage.

There are quite a lot of remains left and it is worth taking the winding path up to see them, as well as to enjoy the wonderful views over Castleton and surrounding countryside.

It is thought the spelling of the name changed in the 19th century when Walter Scott published his novel 'Peveril of the Peak.'

The bases of columns in the castle   **The jakes, or toilet of the castle**   **View from the path as you wind up**

The 'Shivering Mountain'

As well as being overlooked by the castle, the village has a brooding hill looming over it. Known as Mam Tor, or 'The Shivering Mountain', this imposing feature is a result of a huge landslide of shales and sandstones, thousands of years ago. The result looks a bit like a quarry. The average movement of the landslide is thought to be about 25 centimetres a year, more if it is very rainy.

Over many years, as the rock layers crumbled and led to the land slips, the movement earned the hill the name of shivering mountain. The A625 road used to run along the base of the hill but kept slipping, so in 1979 the road was closed, making Winnats Pass once again the only road out of Castleton to the West.

It is still possible to walk along the remains of the road and see the damage it suffered, which makes it look as though there has been an earthquake.

The other name, 'Mam Tor' is thought to mean 'mother mountain or rock' in the Celtic language. Maybe this is because it was breast shaped or maybe because, as Defoe surmised, **"the soft crumbling earth, which falls from the summit of the one, breeds or begets several young mountains below."**

Mam Tor was also once home to a late Bronze or early Iron age hill fort. It is easy to see why it was chosen as a defended lookout. From the top of Mam Tor there are some wonderful scenic views so it is worth going up there if you can. There is a walk along footpaths downhill back to Castleton, via Hollins Cross.

Also dominating this landscape are the twin peaks of Lose Hill and Win Hill. Win Hill is the pointy one that looks a little like a volcano or a badly baked bun.

These two hills are in local folklore associated with a battle between Edwin, King of Northumbria and a pagan King of Mercia, around the 7th century. The victors are said to have camped on the peak now known as Win Hill, though this may be a later bit of romanticism .

A view of Mam Tor, through the main street of Castleton

"A lyric in limestone"

Winnats Pass is a dramatic gap in the limestone cliffs to the west of the village. The name was once written 'wyndeyates' – meaning 'the pass through which the wind sweeps'.

It was originally an old saltway and many tired men and animals would have wound their laden way down the forbidding hill into the town from Cheshire, without the benefit of the tarmac which lines it today.

We get a lovely description of Winnats in a book called 'All About Derbyshire' by Edward Bradbury, which was written in 1884. In the chapter 'A Cruise Around Castleton' he says:

"the green of clinging verdure and the gloom of changing shadows....It is a romance in rock; a petrified poem; a lyric in limestone."

Murder most foul

One of the enduring tales in the history of this pass is that of a terrible deed, when in 1758 two people were slain there.

The victims were two wealthy lovers - thought to be called Allan and Clara, who had eloped and were on their way to Peak Forest – a Derbyshire equivalent of Gretna Green.

In Winnats Pass they were waylaid by five miners from the Odin Mine, intent on harm and profit. The couple were led to a barn which then stood near Speedwell Cavern and there the miners killed them both with pick axes. They stole their possessions and buried the bodies nearby.

The crime was soon discovered when the horses of the victims were found wandering alone, but the bodies were not found until ten years later and buried in St. Edmund's graveyard.

Though the murderers were never caught, destiny seems to have handed out its own justice. One of them fell to his death from near the murder spot, another was killed by a mysterious falling rock in the same place, a third went mad and tried to kill himself, dying a miserable death. The fourth hung himself. It was the fifth miner who finally admitted the deed on his deathbed.

What is believed to be the unfortunate Clara's side saddle is now to be seen at Speedwell Cavern.

Again Edward Bradbury puts the event into words well:

"Two runaway lovers, as rich in money as in love, returning from a matrimonial visit to the Peak Forest Parson.. are on horseback on their happy way Hallamshire-ward.

"In the gloomy pass of the Winnats are a band of murderers, who waylay them and still their warm hearts forever, simply for the sake of their personal possessions....

"The place is supposed to be still haunted by the victims of the tragedy. When the winter wind screams down the narrow pass on a wild night, local superstition associates the weird sound with the death-cry of the lovers and shiveringly cowers under the bedclothes."

Looking up the stunning natural feature of Winnats Pass, framed by boughs on rowan trees at the bottom

An ancient ritual

A strange ceremony takes place in Castleton on the evening of 'Oak Apple Day'- May 29th - usually around 6pm.

The event is called the Garland Day Ceremony and has been celebrated in Castleton for centuries.

It may originally have been some kind of fertility rite, perhaps on May 1st, but was later adapted and absorbed in the 17th century into another event – that of Oak Apple Day – celebrating the restoration of King Charles II to the throne in 1660.

Oak Apple Day was celebrated by wearing an acorn or oak spray in honour of the fact that it was an oak tree in which King Charles hid from Parliamentary forces.

Combining these with a May Day spring fertility festival could be where all the flower tradition on this Oak Apple day began. Some of the people in the procession on Garland Day still carry sprigs of oak today.

it is quite appropriate that the two festivals could be combined, as Charles' return to the throne indeed ended wat could be seen as the 'winter' of the Puritan ban on dancing and May Day festivities. So it was a good reason to celebrate!

The Garland Ceremony involves a cone shaped frame of wood, about one metre (3ft) high. This is covered in straw and bunches of wild flowers are tied on to cover the straw.

A smaller wreath of flowers, known as the Queen's wreath or posy, is placed on the top.

The completed structure weighs about 25kgs (56 pounds). It is hoisted on to the shoulders of the person who is to represent the king, who is dressed in Stuart period costume.

The upper body of this 'King' is then covered in a mass of flowers so he looks like a floral display, with legs, on horseback. He also resembles a 'green man', such as those seen at May Day ceremonies like Hastings.

The flower bedecked 'king' then tours the village on his horse, starting at a local pub and ending at the market square by the church.

He is accompanied by his 'consort'. The consort or queen is now a woman also dressed in Stuart costume, but used to be played by a man until the 1950s.

The procession is accompanied by a band playing a special Garland Tune, which sounds a bit like the Cornish Floral or Furry Dance.

After this procession, the Queen's wreath is placed on the war memorial and the King is relieved of his Garland.

The garland is then hoisted up to the top of the tower of St Edmunds Church, where it is left to wither.

In the market place there is maypole dancing and singing.

■ **The Castleton Information Centre contains a display of Garland memorabilia.**

If Oak Apple Day falls on a Sunday, the ceremony is held on the Saturday (28th May).

A view along the main street in Castleton

A quiet spot in Castleton, perfect for feeding the ducks!

Castleton Information Centre

Some of the collection of models by Randolph Douglas

This centre is packed with some fascinating displays, tourist information and exhibits. In here you can find an old stone head labelled as Brigantia, which dates to about 1000 BC and was found in a garden wall in Castleton. It is thought to be made by the old tribal inhabitants of Mam Tor, the Brigantes.

Also here is a display about the local man Randolph Douglas who had a 'House of Wonders' in a cottage in Castleton in the 1920s. It was sixpence (2.5p) to see the wonders he had collected. He was a skilled model maker and an amateur escapologist and magician. Harry Houdini helped him with his knowledge of escapism and collection of locks.

Other exhibits at the Centre include costumes and details of the Garland Ceremony and a model of how the castle would probably have looked before it became a ruin.

■ Castleton Information Centre, Main Street, Castleton, Hope Valley S33 8WP ■ Telephone: (01433) 620679 ■ Email: castleton@peakdistrict.gov.uk

Stone head at the Centre

A literary monster

The Terror of Blue John Gap is a bone chilling story written by the creator of that famous detective Sherlock Holmes, Sir Arthur Conan Doyle. It features in his book 'Tales of Terror and mystery' penned in 1929.

The tale tells of one Dr James Hardcastle, from London, staying in the Derbyshire hills to regain his health whilst lodging with two old maids He hears tales of a monster that sneaks from the cave depths at night to kill the sheep and is terrifying the locals:

"Well Doctor." said he, you're not afraid anyhow."

"Afraid!" I answered. "Afraid of what?"

"Of it." said he, with a jerk of his thumb towards the black vault., "of the Terror that lives in the Blue John Cave."

To investigate, the doctor explores the cave, Blue John Gap, described as *"a clean cut arch in the rock, the mouth all overgrown with bushes."*

Whilst near it he hears *"a distant roaring of immense volume"* but puts it down to the *"strange reverberations which come out of an underground water system running amid the chasms of a limestone formation."*

He gets lost in the cavern trying to explore and hears a creature walking within it. When he manages to find his way to daylight he tells the local accademic, but is not believed and he is just given an appointment to a 'Mr Picton at Castleton'- the 'mad doctor' – which he doesn't take up.

Stalking the strange creature again later, Hardcastle sees roaming the dark

"something with rough and bristling hair of a withered grey colour.. the huge body supported upon short, thick, curving legs.... He had reared up on his hind legs as a bear would do, and stood above me, enormous, such a creature as no nightmare had ever brought to my imagination...a shudder of horror passed over me as I observed that the eyes which glistened in the glow of my lantern were huge, projecting bulbs, white and sightless."

Conan Doyle lived in Sheffield for a short while and perhaps got his inspiration whilst visiting the dark and ominous caverns of Castleton, with just candlelight to brave the gloom, wondering just what might live down there...

A place for all seasons

Even during the winter, Castleton is a popular spot. The Castleton Christmas lights have now become an established trip on the tourist calendar, with many coaches turning up to see the twinkling Christmas trees lining the buildings and a horse drawn coach clip-clopping along the street. Santa and carols complete the picture and the castle, as ever, stands watching over it all in silence.

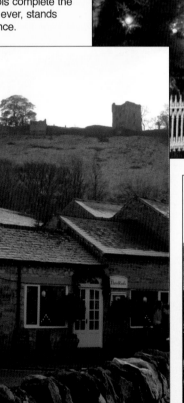

Castleton at Christmas (above and left) and in Summer

Rudely named and awesome

Underneath the castle is a huge, natural rock cavern, said to be the largest natural cave entrance in Britain and the second largest in the world. It is approximately 100ft wide and 60ft high.

Walking up to this cavern is awe-inspiring. The rock faces towering around you look as if they are viewed through a fish eye lens, and birds wheel above in a sky framed by the trees that cling to the edges up by the castle.

As you see the dark hole before you it is like approaching a gateway into the underworld and it is easy to see why caverns were thought to be inhabited by evil spirits.

Indeed, this hole in the rockface that seems to plunge to the nether regions of the earth has associations with nether regions of a different sort – those belonging to the lord of the underworld or hell. It was nicknamed the Devil's Arse. This name came about because of the rather flatulent noises that sometimes emanate from the cavern – due to the water swirling in its bowels, so to speak! Later it also became known as Peak Cavern, out of politeness, but now goes again by that earlier, more evocative, but less delicate name.

The cavern has been one of the tourist must-sees of the area for centuries and was visited by many of the earliest travel writers, painters and literary people.

An early writer about the cavern was Gervase of Tilbury, in 1211. He tells a tale of how a shepherd ventured into the cavern one winter's day in search of his lost sow. As he walked into the darkness he emerged into another land, where it was warmer, with brooks and lakes and people were reaping the harvest. He found his sow and found his way back to the winter of Derbyshire. Daniel Defoe, writing in his book 'A Tour Through England and Wales', did not give this legend much credence:

"Who this shepherd was, how he got into that pleasant country; and above all how he came back to tell the story, our friend Gervase forgot, it seems, to take any notice of; and so the tale is broken off before it was half told."

Looking up to the entrance of Peak Cavern

"All this country is hollow. Could you strike it with some gigantic hammer it would boom like a drum."
Sir Arthur Conan Doyle
(The Terror of Blue John Gap)

Looking out from the entrance of Peak Cavern, The Devil's Arse, showing the ticket office and rope making equipment

Peeks at the Peak

As visitors enter the cavern, the temperature drops. Tiny blind shrimps can sometimes be spotted in the pools of water.

Before the cavern was made more accessible for today's travellers, the only way to get through was to do part of the journey in a coffin-like wooden boat. Also, when these earlier visitors came to the cavern, they did not have the benefit of electricity to pierce the blackness as they set forth. They were sold two tallow candles. Miners used to use candles melted on to the rim of their 'Bradder' hats. (These hats got their name as they were used and made in the village of Bradwell). Visitors were also given piggy backs by the guide over the wet parts of the cavern floor.

A 'Beggars banquet' was held in the main cave of the cavern in 1621. This inspired the poet and dramatist Ben Jonson (1572-1637) to pen a tale of the 13th century highwayman Cock Lorel, the last known king of the beggars, in his work **The Gypsies Metamorphos'd.** In this masque, in the Ballad of Cock Lorel, one of the Gypsies tells his version of how the cavern got the rather rude nickname, when Cock Lorel invited the devil to a feast in the cavern and gave him lots of food:

> *"From the famous Peake of Darby and the Devills arse hard by, where we yearly keepe our musters, Thus th' Aegiptians throng in clusters'*
>
> Ben Jonson, The Gypsies Metamorphos'd.

"All which he devour'd, he then for a close,
Did for a full draught of Darby call.
He heav'd the huge vessell up to his nose,
And left not till he had drunke up all.
Then from the table he gave a start,
Where banquet and wine were nothing scarce
All of which he flirted away with a fart.
From whence it was called the Devill's Arse".
"And there he made such a breach with the winde
The hole too standinge open the while,
That the scent of the vapour before and behind
Hath foulye perfumed most part of the isle".

Another famous writer, the poet and romancer Lord Byron brought one of his many sweethearts to view the caven and described the visit in his memoirs in the early 1820s:

"with the rock so close upon the water – as to admit the boat only to be pushed on by a ferry-man (a sort of Charon), who wades at the stern stooping all the time"* Byron also wrote: *"there are things in Derbyshire as noble as in Greece or Switzerland"* (*Charon was a spectral figure who ferried the dead across the River Styx into the underworld, Hades. A custom was to place a coin in the mouth of a corpse to pay for the ferry journey).

From the early 1840s, reaching the 'Great Cave' chamber by boating through the naturally formed eyehole and tunnel became unnecessary. A footway was laid across the 'First Water' and a few yards of rock excavated. This way in now requires stooping for about 20 paces under the low roof and has earned the name 'Lumbago Walk.'

From here the tour emerges into the huge chamber. Lighting is added now but in earlier times the impenetrable darkness would be lit by flares. Added entertainment was then provided by choirs of unseen children, who scuttled into place in a higher part of the cave, their way lit by hand held tapers, singing as visitors entered.

The public tour ends at The Devils Staircase. Beyond that is 13 miles of cave system for those intrepid cavers with expertise and a sense of adventure to explore. In the depths below can be heard the swooshing waters of the River Styx. Should it ever become silent, floodwaters may slowly be rising and at Lumbago Walk the guide may modify the tour according to conditions, so there is never any risk of flooding for the visitors.

On the cave walls at this point can be seen names of previous visitors who damaged it with their carvings. One name is said to have been added by Lord Byron. There can indeed be seen the name Byron(e), though as it is written with an 'e' on the end, perhaps it was in a mood of artistic spelling variation on his part!

■ Peak Cavern, The Devil's Arse. Castleton. Tel: 01433 620285
■ email: info@peakcavern.co.uk ■ www.devilsarse.com

Rope making in the Peak Cavern

During the mid 17th century the imposing entrance to the Peak Cavern was inhabited by ropemakers. They lived and worked there, supplying rope for Castleton's lead mining industry.

By the 19th century this industry had all but vanished and the rope making needs much lessened, so the community whittled away.

The ropemaking tradition in the village still carried on however- as until 1969, every woman married in Castleton was given a clothes line as a gift. Not the most romantic symbol of married life but certainly practical!

You can still see demonstrations of rope making today if you take one of the fascinating guided tours of the cavern.

How rope is made

When the community and ropemaking was flourishing, the raw material, hemp, would arrive on packhorses.

The hemp was twisted by hand into larger hunks 3ft (1m) long, called 'streaks' which were then combed to get rid of knots - a process called 'hackling'.

When hackled these streaks were then tied around the waists of the ropemakers, who took it to the 'rope walk'.

On here the ropemaker attached one end of the streak to a stand and walked backwards, twisting the streaks anti-clockwise as they went. This produced a long, chunkier piece of hemp called a 'yarn'. Lengths of yarn were spliced together, usually by children. This yarn was hung, over a high pole, with a weight attached to stretch it. When it became stretched enough it was wound onto a large drum.

Right are some of the wooden tools used by ropemakers, including tops, cones and noosing horns. The drawing is of a noosing horn

High poles with weighted yarn hanging from them
← Yarn
Weight
Drums with yarn wound around

Above are poles with the weighted yarn hanging from them. The yarn is then wound onto the drums

Rope making in the Peak Cavern

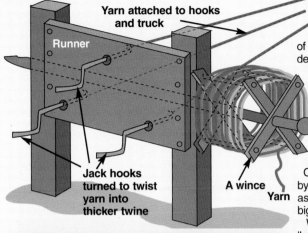

Yarn attached to hooks and truck

Runner

Jack hooks turned to twist yarn into thicker twine

A wince

Yarn

A runner in the cavern, with stools for those operating the runner to take a rest!

On the sled

Top part of sled

Spinner turns and enables the twine hooked on it to twist into one rope

Twine (twisted yarn)

The twine strands are twisted together into one rope

Top or cone moves up the rope as the strands are twisted together

Direction of movement

Sled on its wheels moves forward as rope twists together getting shorter

Diagrams are modified from Peak Cavern display sketches

On the right is a photograph of ropemaker Bert Marrison in his later years, tying a Marrison loop. In the circle is a picture of his last resting place in the cavern, with a candle burning by it

The twisted yarn is then removed from the wheel and put onto a structure called a 'wince'. This is placed on a ***runner*** - a frame fitted with three hooks which stands at one end of the rope walk.The length of rope it is possible to make is determined by the length of the rope walk.

The other end of the rope is attached to a weighted '**sled**', that is fitted with swivelling 'jack hooks' and wheels. These wheels enable the sled to creep forward as the swivelling hooks are turned, twisting the three hooked pieces of yarn and so shortening them as they twist to make thicker twine. The strands that are put on to the hooks are rubbed with tallow (animal fat) to make them easier to handle (as they have less friction) and also more waterproof.

On the sled, the other end of the three strands are kept apart by a wooden item called a top, or cone. This cone is moved up as the strands of twine are then twisted together into one bigger, thicker rope.

When the rope is finished, it is taken off the sledge and a 'looper' is put in the end. The rope is then put on to one hook and then wound clockwise to tighten it and make it stronger.

The end of the rope still has loops and so would unwind if left. A 'noosing horn' is used to push the ends through a loop and secure it. A 'Marrison loop' is the name given to the method of finishing the rope. It was invented by a ropemaker called Abraham Marrison.

An ancestor of Abraham Marrison was the last ropemaker to work in the cavern. His name was Bert Marrison and he worked in the cavern, returning part-time after retirement until his death in 1983. His ashes are interred there, by a plaque and a candle burning in his memory.

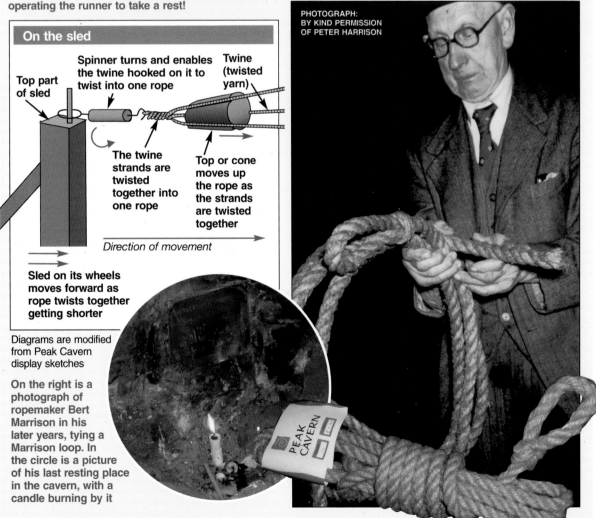

PHOTOGRAPH: BY KIND PERMISSION OF PETER HARRISON

PEAK CAVERN

Other caverns to visit

The Speedwell Cavern, at the foot of Winnats Pass. Also shown are items from the display cabinets in the Speedwell Cavern gift-shop. including the side saddle of the woman who was murdered in Winnats Pass

Speedwell Cavern

This cavern is set at the foot of the spectacular Winnats Pass. It has 105 steps down from the almost hidden cavern entrance and at the bottom a journey on a boat awaits you.

From the landing stage where you begin the trip on to an underground canal, the guide will take you through the old workings of a 200 year old lead mine.

Gliding on the underground waters it is only too easy to imagine the hard working conditions the miners endured.

At 'Halfway House' the canal splits into two, thus enabling boats to pass each other.

On the journey you will see a large cathedral-like cavern and also a subterranean lake which is named rather scarily the 'Bottomless Pit'.

There is also a fascinating display of objects in glass cases at Speedwell Cavern, in the gift shop. These include items made from Blue John, photographs of celebrity visitors to the site and also a saddle said to have been owned by a woman who was murdered by robbers, along with her lover, in Winnats Pass, around 1758.

■ For visits or more information, contact:
Speedwell Cavern Ltd. Winnats Pass, Castleton, Hope Valley, Derbyshire S33 8WA
Telephone: (01433) 620512
Web site: www.speedwellcavern.co.uk

Blue John Cavern

This cavern is up at the top of the hill and is reached from Castleton by either walking up the hillside or by going up Winnats Pass (pictured right), then down the old Mam Tor Road. Like Treak Cliff this mine is a mixture of man made and natural. It is home to eight of the fourteen known varieties of Blue John.

The mineral is still mined here in the winter months and made into jewellery and ornamental objects at the Blue John craft shop in the centre of Castleton.

Blue John can be seen in situ, as well as old mining equipment and stalactites and stalagmites. On the guided tours are seen the Waterfall Cavern, Variegated and Grand Crystallised Caverns as well as Lord Mulgrave's Dining Room, where miners were entertained. There is a Cavern Shop selling gifts and light refreshments.

■ For visits or more information, contact: **Blue john Cavern, Castleton, Hope Valley S33 8WP**
Telephone: (01433) 620638 or (01433) 620642 (craft shop)
www.bluejohn-cavern.co.uk www. bluejohn.gemsoft.co.uk

Treak Cliff Cavern

Blue John was discovered here as miners were exploring the cave system for lead. Miners in the 1750s dug tunnels by hand to reach the minerals.

Formations to be seen at Treak Cliff include the Blue John Stone Pillar (the largest piece still in situ) and The Stork.

There are also fossils to see, as well as the Dream Cave and Fairyland, full of what are perhaps the finest stalactites and stalagmites you'll see in the Peak District. There are also the Witch's Cave and Aladdin's Cave.

The Blue John seen on the visitor routes at the cavern is now preserved, but Treak Cliff still mines Blue John from sites visitors don't see and it is made into small bowls, jewellery and other decorative items.

There is also a gift shop which was established in 1949, selling these items and others in the centre of the village.

■ **For visits or more information, contact: Treak Cliff Cavern, Castleton, Hope Valley S33 8WP**
■ **Telephone: (01433) 620571**
■ **www.bluejohnstone.com**

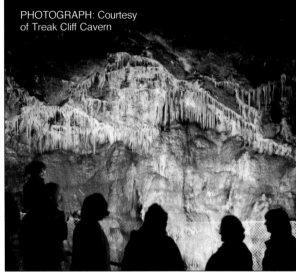
PHOTOGRAPH: Courtesy of Treak Cliff Cavern

Formations in Treak Cliff Cavern. Above is Fairyland and below is The Stork with stalactites and stalagmites

Mam Tor

Treak Cliff Cavern entrance, high on the hill near Mam Tor

PHOTOGRAPH: Courtesy of Treak Cliff Cavern

Stalactites and stalagmites

StalaCtites point down from the Ceiling

StalaGmites point up from the Ground

These 'icicles' found in caverns are made when the soft rock limestone dissolves in rainwater. Rainwater is a very dilute form of carbonic acid as it has absorbed carbon dioxide from the air. This water containing the dissolved limestone (calcium carbonate) seeps into the caverns. Tiny particles of the limestone then accumulate as water falls to the floor.

Over the centuries the particles build up and get longer, forming the icicle shapes, called **stalactites.**

The best rate of drip for forming stalactites is thought to be about 4 to 7 drops of water per hour. Many drip much more slowly than that. The average growth rate of stalactites is about 1mm every 65 years. That suggests that the ones in Treak Cliff Cavern are thousands of years old.

As the water drips down, more limestone particles build up on the floor to form points in the other direction, upwards. These are **stalagmites.** One way to remember which is which is stalaCmites, with the **C** standing for ceiling and stalaGmites -with the **G** standing for ground.

Sometimes the stalactites and stalagmites grow large enough to meet up in the middle and form a column.

Blue John

Edward Bradbury, in the opening lines of 'A Cruise Around Castleton' waxes lyrical about the famous mineral to be found in the caverns there:

"A bit of Blue John spar! I use it as a paper-weight. It must be dismissed from that office, It has such a tendency at times to catch my eye and send me wandering off on the wings of Memory...up to Peveril's Castle in the Peak."

Blue John is a form of the mineral Fluorite (calcium fluoride). The word comes from the latin **fluere** – to flow – as it was often used as a flux. Fluorite is the name given to the mineral, but fluorspar is the name given to the the fluorite ore which is mined and processed.

Items made from Treak Cliff Cavern Blue John

Discovery of the Blue John form of the mineral is often attributed to the Romans. They could have been the first to see it as they had a fort at Brough, not far from Castleton and mined lead in the area, though no one is sure.

This mineral can come in many forms and pure fluorite is colourless and transparent. The type with bands of bluish-purple and white-yellow bands is the one which has come to be known as Blue John. No one is yet quite sure what causes the colouration. It has long been known that the colour can be made to disappear with heating and some craftsmen heat the mineral to make it a little paler for more variation.

The origin of the name is uncertain and was not well known until about the 1760s. Some say it was so called by the miners, to distinguish it from Black Jack, their name for zinc ore or sphalerite. Another explanation is that the name comes from the corruption of the French words **'bleu et jaune'** (blue and yellow). Before this name seems to have stuck it was sometimes called **Derby Drop or Derbyshire Spar.**

Every vein has its own signature pattern however and those who study it can tell just by looking where a piece of the mineral is mined from.

The early miners used 'fire setting' to extract the mineral. A wood fire was built against the limestone and left to burn overnight. The rock expanded with the heat and when the miners returned they threw a bucket of cold water over the area, which cooled it rapidly and so cracked the rock with the sudden difference tin temperature. Wedges were then put in the resulting cracks to split it further.

Another method used was 'lime blasting' in which holes were drilled in the rock and packed with lime. The lime was then wetted and it expanded, which cracked the rock.

Once mined, by whatever method, the mineral has to be left for months to thoroughly dry out. It is then heated and resin added to harden it. Once it was pine resin that was used but today it is a synthetic form. The mineral can then be shaped on grindstones for jewellery or by turning on a lathe for ornaments. There was once a trend to fit Blue John into elaborate gold coloured fittings such as vase handles. These gold fittings were called **ormolu** from French words for gold (or) and **molu** (grinding or moulding).

Tourism at Castleton developed over the decades and shops selling Blue John were popular in Buxton, Matlock Bath and of course Castleton. Blue John is still a popular gift with tourists to the area today, though mining of it is restricted.

Although this blue-purple banded form of fluorite is unique to Derbyshire, there are also similarly coloured deposits in China, Nevada and Iran. These, however, don't have the same unique inclusions as Blue John.

Fine examples of the use of Blue John are the fireplaces by 18th century designer/architect Robert Adam, at Kedleston Hall near Derby (National Trust). There are also fine collections to be seen at Chatsworth, Windsor Castle, Lauriston Castle near Edinburgh and many museums, including Sheffield, Birmingham, Derby and the Natural History Museum, London. Much of the collection in the Sheffield museum was damaged in the Blitz in World War II. The collection once belonged to Erasmus Darwin, grandfather of famous naturalist Charles Darwin.

"Everything from shells"

The Peak District is a good place to find fossils. It is hard to visualise such areas as Winnats Pass as being underwater, but once it was under a warm sea, full of life that later became preserved in rock.

Palaeontology is the study of fossils.

The word fossil comes from the Latin word meaning 'dug up' and once was used to describe anything that could be dug up by a spade, including metals, bones etc.

Today we have a more specific meaning for the word – what we call fossils are the remains or traces of prehistoric lifeforms that are preserved in rock, or their impressions that are so preserved.

Around 300 million years ago, in an era known as the Carboniferous, the White Peak was under a sea. Living creatures such as those called brachiopods (a bit like cockle shells) and crinoids (screw like) lived there and it is these that are often seen in the fossils found in the area now.

As the sea creatures died they fell to the sea bed and their bones and shells, full of calcium, gradually compressed together into what later became limestone rock.

This pale rock is the carboniferous limestone which forms the White Peak and earns it the name.

In many places around the White Peak, as you wander, you can spot these ancient sea creatures in rocks and stone walls.

Good places to see fossils in the Peak are Winnats Pass, Cavedale, Peak Cavern, Treak Cliff Cavern, Lathkill Dale and Millers Dale.

Erasmus Darwin

Erasmus Darwin was a doctor, inventor and poet, as well as being a pioneer of evolution like his grandson, the famous Charles Darwin.

Erasmus was born near Newark and went to school in Chesterfield. He later became a doctor at Nottingham and Lichfield. He was also head of the 'Lunar Society' of Birmingham. This was a group of brilliant 18th century thinkers and experimenters who met every month on the Monday night nearest the full moon. Other society members were Matthew Boulton, James Watt, (of steam engine fame), potter Josiah Wedgewood and chemist Joseph Priestley.

The Lunar Society loved all the history geology etc to be found in the Peak District. Erasmus visited Treak Cliff at Castleton In the 1770s. The story goes that when he was in one of the caverns, he slipped on the wet cavern floor and, as he did, clutched at the rock sides. As he did so he noticed the ancient and tiny creatures fossilised in the limestone.

Soon after he added a motto to the family crest: **"E conchis omnia'** (Everything from shells), as well as three scallop shells. He pondered that all life has descended from these our tiny ancestors now remaining trapped in rocks. This incident, and the following musings, perhaps started the great theories of evolution, competition and survival fermenting in his mind that later Charles became famous and controversial for.

Even when Erasmus painted his new motto with the shells on his carriage there was controversy. He was accused of the symbol being blasphemous by one Canon Seward, his friend living in nearby Eyam at the time, who said it gave the impression that the world was created by accident and not by God.

Two views of the scenery around Castleton.
Top is a view towards Mam Tor from the castle.
Bottom is a view from the road walking up to Winnats Pass

Odin Mine

Just along from the Blue John tourist traps at Treak Cliff is this moody and scenic spot, once full of hard working miners, probably too exhausted to appreciate the lovely views...

Odin Mine is one of the oldest mines in Derbyshire, overlooking the picturesque village of Castleton and under the shadow of the shivering mountain Mam Tor.

An old workplace

This now quiet spot above Castleton is often a detour for walkers enjoying the scenery as they make their way.

Once though, the people striding down the path would have been on the way to a backbreaking day's work in the dark, sun starved depths, to dig out the lead ore.

The dark mouth in the left of the hillside just past the popular Treak Cliff caverns is the entrance to what is probably the oldest lead mine in Derbyshire, Odin Mine.

Again the novelist Edward Bradbury gives us an evocative description:

"The Odin Mine, again, an old obsolete lead-working, is interesting because of its historic renown.
The Romans worked the lead; and in Saxon times the place became local Siberia to which prisoners were sentenced to labour out their lives at the mines."

The workings are deep and dangerous and not entered by even experienced potholers and cave explorers.

Across the road from the cave entrance is the iron crushing ring and millstone from the mine, still in the original position. The mine is now in the care of The National Trust.

Odin

The cave takes its name from Odin, the Norse god of wisdom, war and death. He was the principal god, seen as the ancestor of kings.

He was also known as Woden to the Anglo-Saxons.

Odin tried many things to expand his power and knowledge. He wounded himself with his own spear and hung himself from the mythical tree at the centre of the world, the ash tree Yggdrasil, with its roots in the earth and its branches in the heavens.

Above: The Odin Mine crushing circle and a small copper butterfly spotted whilst sitting there

He hung there for nine days and nine nights a kind of voluntary sacrifice and rejuvenation that has been compared by some to Christ's death and resurrection. His reward was the knowledge of the runes; characters carved on stones or wood that were used as writing, but also had a magical meaning or power.

Another of his feats to become the `All Wise' was to manage to drink at the Well of the Highest Wisdom. This was guarded by the giant Mimir, at the roots of Yggdrasil. The water gave the drinker much knowledge and wisdom.

The price Odin forfeited for being allowed to drink was his right eye. Hence Odin is usually depicted as a one eyed, middle aged man, with a long beard and a spear, as his principal weapon. He is often shown wearing a long cloak and a wide brimmed hat. He roamed the land dressed like this, disguised as a simple traveller, to observe the ways of men.

Another of his legends reminds of a more recent literary story given to us by Tolkein... Whilst Odin was hanging on the world tree his ring, Draupner, dropped eight magic rings of equal value every ninth night.

In Scandinavian myth there are more surviving stories about him. He lived in Valhalla and was often depicted with a breast-plate helmet and spear, made for him by the dwarves. Odin also had companion black ravens, called Thought and Memory.

The fourth day of our week still reminds us of this ancient god as it is named after him, Wodin's day (Wednesday). The French call Wednesday Mercredi – Mercury's Day, after the god Mercury

A close up of the crushing circle and millstone

MAM TOR
Odin Mine Crushing Circle
Odin Mine
Blue John Cavern
Treak Cliff Cavern
To Buxton
WINNATS PASS
CASTLETON
From Sheffield A625
Speedwell Cavern
Peak Cavern (Devil's Arse)
Peveril Castle

Around Hope

This place with an uplifting name is an ancient one, long a stop on the routes of travellers winding across the Peak...

The impressive parish church of St. Peter, at Hope

The village of Hope lies on the prehistoric route through the Peak District known as the Portway. Packhorses carrying salt and other supplies crossed the Pennines and passed through here. Romans too would have crossed the River Noe here, on their road to the nearby fort at Brough.

A popular spot

Today, Hope is a popular spot, with a historic church and cross, tea shops and pubs. It is also a good place to begin walks or see well dressings. Like nearby Castleton, it stands in the White Peak. Looking over the village are Win Hill and Lose Hill. As mentioned earlier, tradition has it that the names come from a 7th century battle, which took place between Edwin of Northumbria and the Mercian King Penda.

People have lived, worked and worshipped at this spot for many centuries. The church is said to be the oldest recorded Christian place of worship in the northern Peak District.

In Saxon times it was the focus of one of the biggest parishes in England. There was once a Norman (1066-1100AD) castle here, between Pindale Road and Peakshole Water. The castle comprised of a mound and ditch, and stood guard over the river crossing of the old Portway track. It stands on private land now.

When the Midland Railway and the station arrived at Hope in the 1890's and the dams were built at Howden and Derwent, the place got busier and more well known, as well as expanding, with new housing joining the older ones clustered around the lovely parish church of St. Peter.

In the 1920's the cement works, still there today with its 400ft (120m) chimney, was developed, before the area became a National Park. It is a highly visible, if somewhat unaesthetic, landmark in the Hope Valley.

A sign from a walk which leads from Hope, off Castleton Road

PUBLIC FOOTPATH TO LOSE HILL — MAM TOR RIDGE. LEAVE NO LITTER.

The Church

St. Peter's is on a site of worship which dates back to Saxon times. There are traces of Saxon stone in the building and some fabulous gargoyles can be seen on the exterior – including a coyly grinning winged creature that looks like a cartoon, two mouth pullers and one that is somewhat like an evil Yorkshire terrier with wings.

Much of the present building dates to the 14th century. The chancel was rebuilt in 1882 and the east end of the church rebuilt in 1908. Inside can be seen a Norman font, 13th century tomb slabs and a 14th century piscina. There is also a 17th century pulpit. There is more information inside the church, which is locked during the week.

Assorted gargoyles

The word gargoyle comes from the Latin word *'gurgulio'* meaning throat, as their purpose is to spew out rainwater, usually through their throat.

Outside the church

The Market Cross

Opposite the South porch can be seen six octagonal steps that were the base from a medieval cross, with a more recent shaft added on top. It may have originally stood in the market place area.

The Old Hall

This used to be the home of a prominent local family called Balguy. It used to have grounds that spread over the car park and former cattle market.

The circle in the picture above shows the site of the uprights of the old stocks. Below is a close up

Old stocks

Near the north gate of the church (the one on Castleton Road) the tops of the stone uprights of the old village stocks have been set into the wall, low down near the pavement. They were put here when the churchyard was extended in 1887, after some cottages on the site were demolished.

Looking over from the church to The Old Hall, on the corner of Castleton Road and Edale Road

Gravestones at St. Peter's

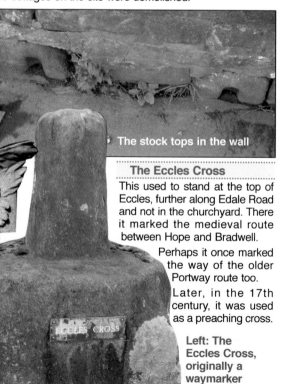

The stock tops in the wall

The Eccles Cross

This used to stand at the top of Eccles, further along Edale Road and not in the churchyard. There it marked the medieval route between Hope and Bradwell.

Perhaps it once marked the way of the older Portway route too.

Later, in the 17th century, it was used as a preaching cross.

Left: The Eccles Cross, originally a waymarker

A view of St. Peter's spire

The location of the celtic face on the wall

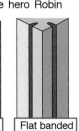

THIS 18TH CENTURY GUIDE POST (CIRCA 1709) WAS FOUND IN 2000 AND PLACED HERE IN SEPTEMBER 2003 BY HOPE HISTORICAL SOCIETY

Old guidestone

This waymarking stone, now set on a stone gatepost, is from the 18th century and was found in the vicargage garden

Celtic face

On the north wall of the tower, below and to the right of the clock, there is a carved face built in to the wall. This is re-used from an earlier building on this site or elsewhere. It is badly eroded now.

The old cross

There is a fine old cross shaft standing near the south porch of the church, next to the main path.

It was found broken into two pieces – one of which was being used as a lintel and one was built into a wall at the old school house. When the school was demolished the pieces were discovered, repaired and sited here.

The type of decoration has led experts to date it to the 11th century. The decoration has units of interlocking knotwork, that is different to the so called 'Peak School' of carving, which has vine scroll decoration.

The sandstone cross is decorated on all faces and features stylised leaf patterns, snakes, concentric circles and some figures. It is well preserved, probably because it was hidden, built into a wall for so long.

Peak District crosses

These have a mixture of Pagan and Christian symbols and the Peak ones seem to be of a similar design or school, which features 'vinescroll' patterns. Any figures tend to have heavy drapery and pierced hole eyes. Also Peak crosses often have an archer figure, (as on the Bakewell Cross and also Sheffield Cross), perhaps a Scandinavian god that was a forerunner of the hero Robin Hood!

Parts of a cross

Square terminal

Round terminal

Armpit

Types of edging found on crosses

Cable	Flat banded	Rolled

Knotwork on the Hope cross (left).

Right is one face which has knot-work, stylised leaves and two figures which appear to be holding a staff or cross

In Hope village

15. Hearse House

At the corner of Eccles Close and Edale Road is a plaque on a wall. It marks the site where an old hearse house built in 1851 once stood. It was a fire station during World War II and was demolished in 1960

14. Methodist Chapel

This was built in 1835 and was extended in 1926

13. Tin Hut

Now a hairdressers, this is perhaps the last surviving hut from the old 'Tin Town' built at Birchinlee for construction workers building the Howden and Derwent Dams

1. St Peter's Church
2. Remains of stocks
3. Eccles Cross
4. Saxon Cross
5. Guidestone
6. Market Cross

12. Old Hall

CASTLETON ROAD

ECCLES CLOSE

EDALE ROAD

STATION RD

PINDALE RD

7. The Castle

Site of Hope Castle, now on private ground

Rules issued in 1947 when impounding stock was falling into disuse

HOPE PINFOLD
Rules for the Pound keeper

Any person impounding an animal or animals is answerable for providing food and water every 12 hours and is liable for a fine of 20/- for neglecting to do so.

The pound keeper is not liable, but it would be best for the pound keeper to make arrangements to feed and water any animal or animals impounded, with the person who has brought the animal or animals to be impounded

The pound keeper cannot refuse to impound any animal brought to him. Animals must not be tied up in the pound

If any animals should receive damage from the pen being unfit for pounding animals. the owner can claim damage from the person who impounded the animal, but the pound keeper is not liable

The pound keeper cannot bring any action if the pound be broken open and the animals liberated by the owner. The person who impounded them must bring the action

The person impounding an animal and having to supply food and water can receive up to double the value of the food and water supplied and to make payment certain can, after 7 clear days, from the day of impounding, sell one or more of the animals to receive the payment of such food and also for the pounding fee and the fine for trespass.

If an animal die in the pound, the impounder is not liable if the animal died through no fault or neglect of his

Before selling an animal to recover the fine etc. for impounding, the impounder must give 3 days notice of his intention to do so. (Public printed notice)

The animal must be sold openly at some public market for the best price it will fetch

Under the Cruelty to Animals Act, if any person who impounded the animal neglect to feed an water it, any person may enter the pound and do so and can receive the cost for such from the owner before he can take it away

11. Daggers House

This is now a private house but was once a pub with a cross daggers sign

10. Loxley Hall

An old hall of 1900

8. The Pinfold

This is found on the right hand side of Pindale Road as you walk down from the parish church. A person called the the Pinner or Pinder was in charge of it. It was used to impound any stray animals found. The rules are listed above left

9. Old School

On this site was an even older school, where parts of the Saxon cross were discovered when it was demolished

Near Hope

THE CHESHIRE CHEESE

At the edge of the village on the Edale Road is the pretty Cheshire Cheese Inn. It is said to get its name from when the *jaggers* or packmen carrying salt along the Portway from Cheshire paid for their lodging with a Cheshire cheese instead of money.

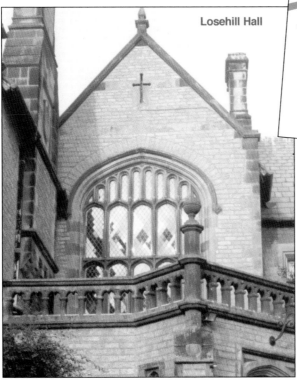

Losehill Hall

LOSEHILL HALL

Just past Hope and just before Castleton on the A625 is the fine old Lose Hill Hall, named after the hill close by. It is now the Peak District National Park Centre for Environmental Education.

It is a traditional Victorian building with modern facilities and stands in 27 acres of parkland, garden and woodland.

The hall has many courses and lectures to choose from and is a lovely environment in which to learn.

■ Losehill Hall, Peak District National Park Centre For Environmenal Learning, Castleton, Hope Valley S33 8WB

■ Telephone: (01433) 620346

■ Email: enquiries.losehill@peakdistrict.gov.uk

■ Fax: (01433) 620346

Brough

Brough Mill

A footpath sign from near Navio Roman Fort

Not far away from Hope is the village of Brough. Here, there is an old corn mill. There has been a mill on this site since around 1200. A water wheel can still be seen there.

There is also a Roman Fort at Brough. It is called Navio or Anavio and was built around 78AD.

It was part of the Roman link between the Roman Melandra fort near Glossop and Templeborough fort in Sheffield, which was built over by the steelworks of the same name .

Brough was a rectangular fort which was abandoned and then later reoccupied and improved. It stands on rising ground at the confluence of the Bradwell Brook and the River Noe.

There have been archaeological digs and finds there over the years.

An altar discovered at Brough was taken to Haddon Hall.

There is not much left to see at Navio on the surface, unless you have a vivid imagination, but it is still worth a visit to stand and daydream of the people who once walked there and in whose footsteps we tread. And maybe even hear echoes of ghostly Italian conversation drifting over the hills.

BRADWELL

This a lesser known and less visited village, just 2 miles from Hope. It is surrounded by the lovely scenery of Bradwell Dale. There are narrow, winding streets, and a 16th century pub – Ye Old Bowling Green.

On the right is a photograph of Bradwell parish church.

Lead mining was once the main occupation of the villagers. The miners wore hats that were a bit like a military helmet and these could have been where the 'tin hat' derived from.

These hats were nick-named 'Bradder Beavers' and they became very popular. A candle stuck in a lump of clay was placed on top of the hat for light when in the darkness of the mines.

Another employer was the cotton mill at Bamford, where many women from Bradwell worked long shifts.

Now the Cement Works is one of the biggest sources of employment in the area.

The tradition of well dressing is still carried out in the village, normally in early August.

For a rainy day...

Samuel Fox, the son of a shuttle maker, was born in Bradwell in 1815. He worked as a 'wire-drawer' in the Rivelin Valley in Sheffield and in Hathersage.

This job, as it sounds, consisted of drawing metal out to make wire. He later took over an old mill and began working for himself, producing pins.

Using his expertise with wire, in the 1880's he invented the steel umbrella mechanism which revolutionised umbrella design, later opening a new factory at Stocksbridge, Sheffield.

The steel replaced the earlier whalebone framework covered with silk to make umbrellas and was much stronger, so it became extremely popular.

The design spread all over the world and the Fox Company expanded over the decades. It is still in production today, under the name Fox Umbrellas Ltd.

The early factory also produced wire stays for corsets and frames for crinolines. It is thought Fox may have invented the umbrella frame whilst wondering what to do with the redundant wire from the crinoline frames when the style went out of fashion.

Fox exhibited products at the London Great Exhibition of 1851. Maybe Joseph Paxton bought an umbrella to keep him dry around the Chatsworth gardens!

On an early Samuel Fox & Company advertisement for umbrellas made at the Stocksbridge works it states

"The new patent umbrella frame, Optimus Paragon... The new improvements...obtain in a remarkable degree such increased strength, with extreme neatness, as to make them the completest frames that have yet been produced. ...

OPTIMUS

"Samuel Fox & Company, convinced that this combination will be found of extreme value in umbrella frames, beg to recommend it with confidence to their friends."

The company adopted a logo with the word OPTIMUS and a running fox.

When nylon was invented, the company quickly saw its potential and replaced the silk previously used on umbrellas with the exciting new material. The new nylon covered umbrella was first introduced in 1947 at the 'Britain Can Make It' exhibition at Crystal Palace in London.

The company have continued to improve and adapt over the decades and produce millions of frames a year.

...and a sunny one!

In Bradwell there is also a place that has been making ice cream since the turn of the century.

The original founder of Bradwell's Traditional Dairy Ice Cream was Grandma Hannah, who made the ice cream in her front parlour in the village. This was quite a task as she had no refrigerator and no electricity. Ice was sent to her by train from Sheffield. At that time the ice cream was sold locally and at nearby areas in the Peak District.

Hannah's grandson Noel Bradwell carried on Hannah's work and ran the business in the 1960's, until it was sold to Lawrence Wosskow in 1992.

Now the ice cream travels further afield and is sold in 16 flavours for catering and cornet outlets and 8 flavours for the 1 litre take home packs. Restaurants, supermarkets and delicatessens now have the brand too. Grandma Hannah would be delighted I'm sure!.

■ **For further information on the product contact:**
Bradwell's Ice Cream, Wortley Court, Bradwell, Hope Valley, Derbyshire S33 9LB
Telephone: (01433) 620536 website: www.bradwells.com

Bagshawe Cavern

This is to the South of the village and takes its name from William Bagshawe of Wormhill, who owned the land.

It was discovered around 1807 by miners working the site, which was then known as Mulespinner Mine. It has a series of caves reached by descending almost 100 steps. Most of the passages are at head height.

Arrangements can be made for parties to visit the caverns.

■ **For details contact: Bagshawe Cavern,**
12 Bradwell Head Road, Derbyshire S33 9HD
■ **Telephone: (01433) 620540**

Bakewell

Most famous for its puddings, markets and a cross, this old 'capital of the Peak' is usually bustling with visitors, browsing shops, exploring the church, or gazing from the historic bridge

The name Bakewell is said to come from the words 'Badecan Wiellon' (Badeca's Well or spring) as the Anglo Saxon Chronicle calls it. Indeed Bakewell owes its expansion to the warm mineral-water springs it was built around. There is evidence of earlier settlements here since at least the Iron Age. By the 12th century, a motte and bailey castle had been constructed on what is still called Castle Hill.

A proud church

Because of its commanding position overlooking the town, the impressive spire of All Saints, the parish church, can be seen from most directions as you wander the shops and take in the ambience of this well loved tourist spot. There has been a church on the site in Bakewell for many centuries, perhaps as early as the late 600s, but almost certainly by the 800s.

The Anglo Saxon church lay at the western edge of the town as the number of cottages and farms clustered around it increased and Bakewell grew in size. The town also grew more prosperous with farming and lead mining.

Between 1100 and 1108 King Henry 1 granted Bakewell and nearby Haddon to William Peveril and it was probably he who took down the Anglo Saxon church and built another, more imposing one, which was probably finished around 1135.

In the 13th century the church was altered and partally rebuilt. The north aisle was widened, the south aisle rebuilt and the Norman arches were replaced by the more pointed ones by then in fashion. By the end of the 13th century there were stalls and misericords (fold up ledges in the choir stalls to give support during long services) and the north and south aisle roofs had been raised. The south transept was lengthened and looked so different it became known as the 'new work' (shortened to Newark).

Many additions and alterations have been made to the church over the decades and a lot of remodelling took place again in the 19th century. In 1825 the, by then, unsafe spire was removed and a few years later the tower, plus bells and clock. Architect William Flockton of Sheffield began rebuilding work in 1841, including a new tower and belfry on a new crossing and finally adding a new spire. All the work and alterations had uncovered Saxon and other very early stones. Many were built into the church walls, others are visible in the porch.

Below: A view over Bakewell and All Saints' graveyard from the church

Around All Saints Church

Spooky stone coffins and a sundial

Walking around the outside of the church you come face to face with a row of eerie, early medieval stone coffins. The hole in the bottom (for the 'juices' to run out?) is a particularly thought provoking touch!. One coffin is thought to be that of a priest, as a pewter chalice was found in it.

As you enter the church, notice the sundial just to the right of the entrance arch. Most of the detail has been worn away over time. The small gnomon (the central peak which casts the shadow) is probably made of brass as it has the characteristic green colour of verdigris, which forms on weathered brass on copper.

The lovely but very worn Noman West door of the church

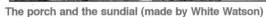

The porch and the sundial (made by White Watson)

Above and right: Two of the doorways of the church, showing very different styles through the ages.

Below: 12th & 13th century Stone coffins line the walls

Saxon and other early stones to be seen in the church porch

There is a large collection of Saxon, Norman and medieval stones to be seen in the porch. An octagonal stone, which has the word MARCUS on it, may have been a Saxon font. (Mark was one of the four evangelists) The grave slabs show symbols for the occupations of the people they once covered, for example chalice (priest), sheep shears and sword.

Right: Stone with the name MARCUS. The evangelist Mark is usually represented by lion, often with wings

The crosses

There are two damaged crosses in the church-yard. A smaller saxon cross shaft (1) (10th/11th century) is by the south path. It was brought to the church after being at Beeley Moor.

The larger Bakewell Cross (2) is a wonderful example of Saxon 8th/9th century workman-ship, with vinescroll work characteristic of Peak District crosses and charming remains of figures. At the bottom of one face, an archer can be seen, similar to that on the old Sheffield Cross.

This cross has a mixture of pagan and Christian imagery on it. On one face is what appears to be a crucifixion, the other face shows a horse and another creature, perhaps a squirrel, lion or monkey, which appears to be eating something.

Close up of one of the carvings, a creature which seems to be eating

Inside the church

The Font

The font dates from the 14th century and has carvings of Christ with John and Mary at either side of him.

Also shown are Peter and Paul, a bishop, a priest and John the Baptist. These figures would originally have been painted. There are traces of a font cover on the top. Fonts were often covered with a lockable lid, this was to prevent people stealing holy water for magic.

The font, which dates from the 14th century and has carved figures

The Chancel

This part of the church has fine examples of 19th/20th century furnishings and stained glass. The mosaic floor has a pattern using symbols of the fleur de lys, (a stylised lily, used to denote the Virgin Mary or the Holy Trinity), chi rho (X and P) which are the first two letters of the word Christ in the Greek alphabet and IHS, which are the first three letters of the name Jesus in Greek.

On the right is a 13th century *sedilia* (stone seats for the clergy) and a double piscina. The choir stalls have medieval wood fragments incorporated into them, with characterful carvings including an acrobat in a rather rude pose (right).

Under the seats are found *misericords*. This word comes from the Latin word 'misercicordia' which means compassion or mercy. These little plinths can give merciful relief to tired feet during long services, by allowing the owner of those feet to rest against them! Carvings on these show many wonderful creations of the artist's mind, including a mermaid and other mythological creatures.

The church has many other fine monuments, such as this one from the 14th century. It is to Sir Godfrey Foljambe and his wife

The Windows

All but one of 1905 are from the mid to late 19th century. They include fine work by the firm Clayton and Bell and also Kempe, whose symbol is a wheatsheaf.

The church's most famous window shows the adoration of the lamb, by the Pre-Raphaelite artist Henry Holiday.

It has the earnest faces and lovingly drawn drapery typical of the style made famous by Morris and Burne Jones.

This window dates from 1893.

Saint George, from the Kempe window of 1905

Floor plan:

CHANCEL

VERNON CHAPEL

NORTH TRANSEPT | TOWER | SOUTH TRANSEPT

NEWARK

NORTH AISLE | NAVE | SOUTH AISLE

SOUTH PORCH

The Newark

This part is the 19th century rebuilding. The Vernon Chapel, the area within the screen, originally had two, maybe three chapels. After the Reformation, it became a chapel for the Vernon and Manners families of nearby Haddon Hall, and holds some lovely 15th-17th century alabaster tombs and ornaments. These tombs would once have been brightly painted and sometimes fragments of colour can be spotted to give an idea of original hues.

One tomb is to Sir George Manners who died in 1623 and his wife Grace, the foundress of Lady Manners School in Bakewell. This school opened in May 1636 as a free school for the boys of Bakewell and Rowsley.

Another fine tomb is that of Sir George Vernon, who died in 1567 and his wives Margaret and Mawde. George was said by the writer Camden to be known by the common folk as 'A petty king in the Peak' because of his fine attire and bearing.

There is also a tomb to George's daughter Dorothy Vernon (she died in 1584) who married John Manners (died 1611).

Margaret, wife of George Vernon, on their tomb

Other notable buildings

The Almshouses

John Manners founded St John's Hospital in 1602. It originally had four dwellings for poor single men of the parish. The almshouses there today were rebuilt in the garden in 1709.

The Old Town Hall

This dates from 1709. It was home to Lady Manners School during the 19th century. It has had many uses in the past, including fire station, shops and administrative centre. It is also thought to be where the town stocks once stood.

Old Market Hall

A lovely building, one of Bakewell's earliest. It was built during the 1600's, with later additions. It now houses the National Park Tourist Information Centre.

The Rutland Arms Hotel

Built on the site of an earlier inn, the White Horse, The Rutland Arms opened in 1805 and was where many coaches stopped and changed horses at the fine coaching stables there. The proprietors then were one Willam Greaves and his wife Ann.

The Old House museum

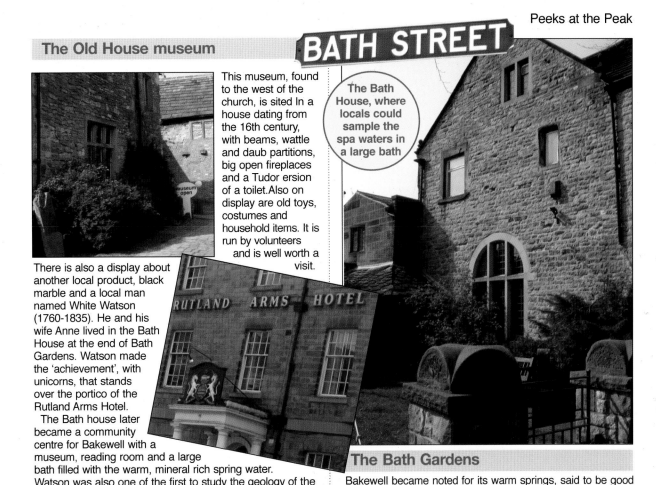

BATH STREET

This museum, found to the west of the church, is sited In a house dating from the 16th century, with beams, wattle and daub partitions, big open fireplaces and a Tudor ersion of a toilet. Also on display are old toys, costumes and household items. It is run by volunteers and is well worth a visit.

The Bath House, where locals could sample the spa waters in a large bath

There is also a display about another local product, black marble and a local man named White Watson (1760-1835). He and his wife Anne lived in the Bath House at the end of Bath Gardens. Watson made the 'achievement', with unicorns, that stands over the portico of the Rutland Arms Hotel.

The Bath house later became a community centre for Bakewell with a museum, reading room and a large bath filled with the warm, mineral rich spring water. Watson was also one of the first to study the geology of the area and wrote a book called 'The Strata of Derbyshire.'

Other fascinating facts about the area can be found in the museum, including an article from 1905 when an elephant escaped from a circus at an evening performance in Bakewell.

■ Bakewell old House Museum, Cunningham Place North Church Street, Bakewell DE45 1DD
Tel (01629) 813642   www.oldhousemuseum.org.uk

The Bath Gardens

Bakewell became noted for its warm springs, said to be good for the health. The springs produced water at a constant 15 °C. The Romans developed many 'spas' like this around Britain such as those at Buxton and may have developed the ones in Bakewell too. By the 17th century, people were taking of the Bakewell waters regularly. The Bath House (above), is all that is left to show this heritage. The spring here was roofed over in 1697. The gardens were developed by the aforementioned White Watson when he lived there.

The famous pudding

The Bakewell Pudding is a local speciality, which carries the name of the town far afield. Tasting nothing like what is now widely sold as a Bakewell Tart, it is indeed more like a pudding, with very soft texture. There are varying and disputed accounts of how this local pudding came about, though similar types of pudding have been made since Tudor times.

One version tells that this delicacy specific to the Peak was invented by accident, in the 1860s, when Mrs Greaves, (the landlady at The Rutland Arms Hotel) left her cook to make a strawberry tart whilst she was busy preparing for important guests. The cook messed up the recipe and order of ingredients as she was so flustered and what resulted was a new type of sweet pudding. But this tale is somewhat mythical and is thought to have been started much later by an account in a town guide of 1936 by a town clerk named Vernon Cockerton.

Today, it is a topic of debate just who cooks puddings to the original recipe. The exact ingredients remain a closely guarded secret. The pudding Ann Greaves made was likely to have been much plainer than those today, with no ground almonds or almond essence.

The Old Original Bakewell Pudding Shop (right) on Bridge Street is one place that sells the puddings and claims the 'original' recipe.

There is a booklet by local historian Trevor Brighton available at the Old House Museum, that tells more of Mrs Ann Greaves and the Bakewell Pudding.

The Bakewell Pudding Shop on Bridge Street

The old bridge and around

A scene showing the lovely old bridge over the River Wye

The river is a lovely, scenic spot to while away the hours after wandering and enjoying the town.

The Wye at Bakewell has been a major and well defended crossing point for centuries. The bridge above would once have had horses clattering over it, but now has many horseless carriages motoring along the A619 to Chesterfield.

This bridge was originally built around 1300, and was widened on the upstream side in 1828. It has five Gothic arches, with triangular corner stones over the buttresses.

Nearby is an earthwork which is now known as Castle Hill. This is the site of the Norman motte and bailey castle, showing that the area has been an important settlement for a very long time. The castle would have guarded the river crossing.

The entry in the Anglo Saxon Chronicle for 920 mentions Edward the Elder building a 'burh' in Peacland. A burh is an embanked enclosure to act as a base for the soldiers and a safe haven for the local population.

Above: The wild flower cowslip (primula veris) can be seen by the river in April and May

Holme Bridge, for packhorses

Another lovely old bridge is Holme Bridge (above). This is a short distance past the Victoria Mill on Buxton Road.

It is a pack-horse bridge of 1663, just wide enough for one horse to walk across. The low parapets are so that the packs of the horse did not get stuck and could hang over the walls of the narrow crossing.

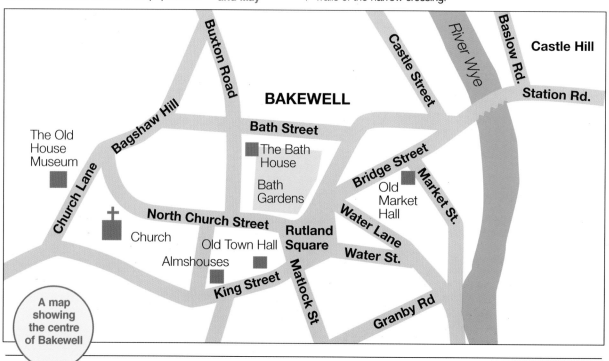

A map showing the centre of Bakewell

Monsal Dale

The huge viaduct at Monsal Head was once the cause of much controversy and opposition, and seen as a great eyesore. Now it has become a popular tourist attraction...

Monsal Head is a fine place to enjoy the beauty of nature, and there are also facilities there for those who wish to walk, cycle, have a meal, a rest, or a pint.

From eyesore to attraction

The dale that we can get such a wonderful vista of at Monsal Head is made from water carving a course through the dome of carboniferous limestone formed around around 300 million years ago. The area was once covered by a warm shallow sea and many of the sea creatures became part of the rock as they died, their bodies sinking into the mud and becoming fossilised.

The huge, 80ft railway viaduct that spans the dale was much opposed by the Victorian writer, artist and critic John Ruskin, who thought it destroyed the beauty of the vale. When it was built he put his thoughts into poetic phrases as a protest and comment:

"That valley where you might expect to catch sight of Pan, Apollo and the muses, is now devasted. Now every fool in Buxton can be in Bakewell in half an hour and every fool in Bakewell at Buxton"

The building of the railway line was also opposed by the Dukes of Devonshire and Rutland, as it went close to their Derbyshire residences. The Duke of Devonshire at Chatsworth refused the line on his lands and a station had to be built at Hassop instead, (This is now a bookstore).

The Duke of Rutland refused a line through his Haddon Hall lands and a compromise was reached, in which the line was built, but hidden in the form of a tunnel.

The line was completed in 1863 and closed 100 years later in the infamous 'Beeching Cuts.'

Nature has softened the man-made structure. The embankments of the viaduct are now clothed in vegetation and the railway cuttings are designated sites of special scientific interest.

At Monsal Head, above the viaduct, is a hotel, public house, tea room and craft shops to peruse and refresh as you admire the stunning view. The paths from Monsal Head up and down into the dale are steep, so you'll need that ice cream at the top to entice you if you go along them!.

The Monsal Trail

The Peak Park authority bought the old railway line and opened it as The Monsal Trail in 1980. The trail follows the path of the old Midland Railway line and for most of the way is also by the side of the beautiful River Wye. It is a little under 9 miles long and runs from just outside Bakewell to just outside Buxton. Part of it is accessible by bicycle. Cycle hire is available at Bakewell Station. You can see the now closed railway tunnels along the route, as well as lovely scenery Footpaths connect the sections that are closed by tunnels.

Two views of the viaduct and one of the old railway tunnels, now closed off

Around the viaduct

Green beauty under the sky

The scene on the right is a view from the viaduct itself, towards Cressbrook. The dale is a lovely place to walk, where cows idle and people cool off in the river on hot days.

Lookng down on the viaduct from the hills above

Left is a tree seen from the path down to the river from Monsal Head. Below, cows idle and chew the grass on the river banks

Fin Cop

From Monsal Head you can see a high peak which is an Iron Age hillfort called Fin Cop. Fin Cop has double bank and ditch fortifications. The inner bank is higher than the outer one.

Remember the child workers

Nearby is Miller's Dale and near there is Litton Mill. Built in the late 18th century, it burned down in 1897 but was rebuilt. This place was once notorious for harsh treatment of its apprentices, some as young as nine and from as far away as London.

Also near Monsal Head is Cressbrook Mill. The original mill was constructed in 1785 by Sir Richard Arkwright. The bigger, main building was opened by a man named William Newton, once Arkwright's agent, in 1815. Child apprentices were treated relatively better there. They were mostly pauper children and Newton had a school built for them.

This mill was in use until the mid 1960's then fell into disrepair. It has now been turned into private apartments.

Cressbrook Mill, in a bad, but quite romantic, state of ruin, before it was renovated and turned into apartments

Ashford in the Water

This picturesque place on the River Wye near Bakewell is most famous for a lovely old bridge that has a place for washing sheep. There is also a fine old church...

The village of Ashford has long been a main crossing point of the River Wye and the river and the bridges over it are major features of this pretty village, which lies just off the main A6 road between Bakewell and Buxton.

Clean sheep!

The main bridge in Ashford is named the Sheepwash Bridge, as it has a pen next to it where sheep could be held whilst ready to be washed in the river, before their wool was shorn. It is a medieval packhorse bridge that has been widened over the years.

There is a village pump (right) near the Sheepwash Bridge, which has an eight sided roof built over it. The Peak District custom of Well Dressing is observed in Ashford.

The bridge at Ashford, with the pen (top) for holding sheep to be washed

Holy Trinity Church

The present church at Ashford was heavily rebuilt in the 1870s and this is the date of most of what we can see today, but there were earlier ones on the site. A Norman one stood here once.

The path running through the church yard has yew trees by it. Yew tree are usually found in graveyards and many are much older than the church whose ground they occupy.

Near the path are the remains of a 15th century preaching cross set on octagonal steps.

Near the churchyard stands an old medieval building called the tithe barn. A 'tithe' was one tenth of a persons produce or earnings which was paid to support the church and clergy. Tithe barns would hold the collected produce

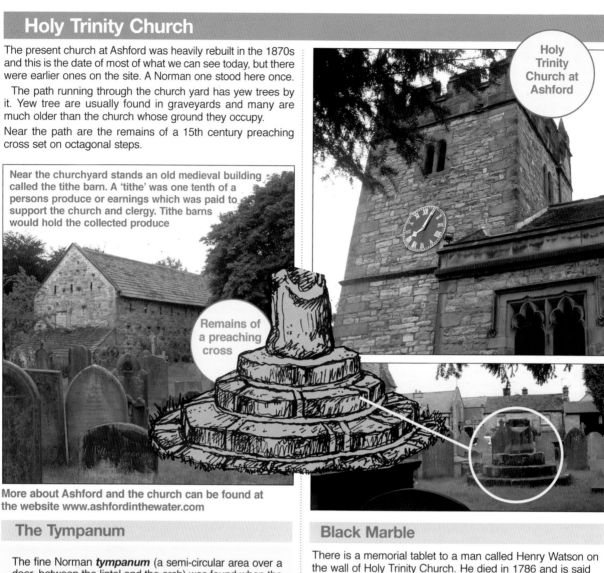

Holy Trinity Church at Ashford

Remains of a preaching cross

More about Ashford and the church can be found at the website www.ashfordinthewater.com

The Tympanum

The fine Norman *tympanum* (a semi-circular area over a door, between the lintel and the arch) was found when the church was having rebuilding work done in 1869-70.

It was discovered built into the south wall and restored to what would have been its original position over the inner church doors. Tympanum are usually highly decorated.

This one shows what looks like a boar (on the left) and a lion or wolf like creature (on the right). They are eating from a tree or plant that is growing between them, with its branches and leaves spreading above.

The scene is thought be some to be a depiction of verses from psalm 80 in the Bible. This psalm tells of a vine out of Egypt that took root and filled the land and:

"boars from the forest ravage it and the creatures of the field feed on it."

A drawing and photograph of the tympanum

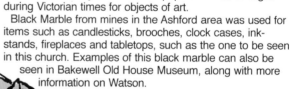

Black Marble

There is a memorial tablet to a man called Henry Watson on the wall of Holy Trinity Church. He died in 1786 and is said to be buried in the churchyard.

The chief industry in Ashford used to be a 'black marble' works established by Henry Watson in 1748. Black Marble was not really a true marble but a finely textured grey limestone.

The marble effect comes from giving it a very high polish. Watson invented machinery and techniques that made it more easy to produce this Ashford Marble and thus made it more commercially available and popular. It was in vogue during Victorian times for objects of art.

Black Marble from mines in the Ashford area was used for items such as candlesticks, brooches, clock cases, inkstands, fireplaces and tabletops, such as the one to be seen in this church. Examples of this black marble can also be seen in Bakewell Old House Museum, along with more information on Watson.

These windows are by the company of Pre-Raphaelite artists Burne Jones and William Morris

Under the tower arch inside Holy Trinity Church stands an octagonal font

It was once moved and used as a garden decoration, but later reclaimed by the church. It was restored as the lower part of the shaft was damaged. On the shaft is a monster/dragon of some sort that seems to be embedded in the stone – with a head coming out on one side and tail on the other. The tail of this beast is knotted and salamanders are often depicted with a knotted tail, so perhaps it is a salamander, as on the font at Youlgreave.

Left is the font, with the knotted tail of the creature carved on it showing (circled). The creature's head (shown in the large circle) is around the other side. Below is a carving from the end of one of the roof beams

Virgin Crants

Pictured are Two of the Virgin Crants in Ashford Church

It was once a custom widely observed at the funeral of a young girl that had never married, to carry 'virgin crants' or 'maidens garlands'.

They used to be made from fresh flowers. A more lasting version was also popular, using a bell shape made of willow, on which were fastened ribbons, flowers and rosettes made of crimped and folded white paper. Sometimes they were painted but most were white.

These were seen as a tribute to the dead woman's chaste and virtuous state at her death. Sometimes a pair of gloves was hung in the middle too, or paper gloves or maybe a handkerchief. The name, age and date of death and sometimes a few words were added by friends relatives or betrothed, or perhaps even the girl herself if she knew she was dying.

The garland was then carried at her funeral.

In churches people used to have their own pew and so the garland would be hung above the pew that belonged to the dead girl's grieving family.

Four of these crants still remain in the church at Ashford, though now inside perspex covers for protection. The oldest one is that of Anne Howard, who died on April 12 1747, aged 21.

Virgin crants are mentioned by Shakespeare, in his play Hamlet.

In Act 5, Scene 1, Hamlet is in the graveyard not long after the famous 'Alas, poor Yorick' skull speech. A priest arrives along with the body of Hamlet's dead love Ophelia and complains about how well she is being treated, even allowed to be given crants:

*"Shards flints and pebbles
should be thrown on her;
Yet here she is allow'd her virgin crants,
Her maiden strewments
and the bringing home
Of bell and burial"*

Magpie Mine

Standing starkly against the skyline, near Sheldon village is the old Magpie Mine. This brooding place was cursed by the grieving widows of men who died there...

This mine is one of the deepest and best preserved lead mines in the region. It has had periods of activity and abandonment over the years, as well as deaths

One for sorrow?

Magpie Mine seems to have an eerie atmosphere. It could be that naming it after the magpie, often depicted as a bird of ill omen, didn't help. Even rhymes we remember today give the magpie a sort of prophetic superstition:

"one for sorrow, two for mirth three for a death four for a birth" or *"one for sorrow two for joy three for a girl four for a boy"*.

The place is also said to be haunted by the spirits of former miners who were killed when a dispute erupted here in the 19th century.

The mine is recorded from around 1740 but probably dates from earlier than that. It was worked, abandoned and re-worked at various times in its history. If anyone discovered an unworked mine they could put a cut or nick on the a wooden beam of the mine. This was a means of claiming or 'nicking; the mine for yourself. It is probably where another name for stealing - nicking - comes from.

In the 1820s and 1830s there were many disputes between the miners of Magpie Mine and those of nearby Maypitts and Red Soil Mines. They argued over a vein of lead, and as they were digging this vein, the miners kept breaking into each others workings.

In 1833. these disputes took a tragic turn. The Magpie miners broke into the Great Redsoil vein – also owned by the Maypitt miners. To drive the rivals away, the Maypitt men lit a fire of straw and tar to smoke them out.

The Magpie men lit fires in retaliation to drive their opposition away – but this fire worked too well.

When the Maypitt/Redsoil miners descended they were overcome with smoke and three of them died.

Twenty-four Magpie men were sent to Derby Assizes for trial. Their lawyer said the Magpie miners had lit their fire in self defence and they were eventually acquitted.

The widows of the three men who had died were not happy with this verdict and were said to have placed a curse on Magpie Mine that has never been revoked. From then on it seems to have been beset with bad luck....

Shafts, gins and windings

Over the years there were periods of working and inactivity and attempts at mining at Magpie Mine but the place never seemed to do much business and was dogged with flooding and accidents – the curse was believed by some to be working.

In 1839, John Taylor, the famous Cornish mining engineer, was brought in to re-open the Magpie Mine and brought some Cornish workers with him. He improved working conditions, as well as deepening the main shaft and installing a Cornish pumping engine and steam winding.

Even with his efforts the flooding problems continued and the mine closed again in 1844.

In 1868 a man called John Fairburn took it over and put in a bigger beam pumping engine. There were still water drainage problems and between 1873-1881 a sough (drainage tunnel) was built. It took these eight years to get from the River Wye near Ashford to the main shaft – just 2km. It was a financial disaster and also emptied the wells at Sheldon, meaning the mine had to pay for new wells too.

The ill fated mine had more attempts made at its veins, but the floods were too problematic and in 1958 it closed for good.

A new use and a historic role

In 1962, Magpie Mine was taken over by the Peak District Mines Historical Society as their Field Centre. The centre is usually open at weekends and on Heritage Days. Members of the public can also visit at reasonable times, but should keep to footpaths due to possible danger of uncapped mine shafts around the area.

At the mine, you can see the remains of the Cornish pumping-engine house and chimney, with the head gear of the mine shaft and winding winches. There are some buildings, including the Agents house and smithy cottage used as the Field Centre. There is also a horse-gin, crushing circles, tram lines and spoil heaps and a powder house.

Interior of the Cornish Engine House. Just in front of the engine house is the main shaft.

Below is steel headgear and a cage from the 1950s

Winding machinery

Above: A round powder house, where the explosives were kept, dates from 1840

Around the site

The building shown left is a winding house of 1869. At the side wall is a cable drum which was used to wind the cage holding the miners up and down the mine shaft

Right: One of the mine shafts, now safely capped with a mesh cover. The method of using stones to line the shaft is called 'ginging'

Above is a reconstructed 'gin' at Magpie Mine. A gin is a horse powered wheel arrangement which was used in early mines to wind the rope up and down the mine shaft. The model of a gin shown below is on display in Castleton Information Centre

A floral indicator

You may see a small white flower in the grass at Magpie Mine. This is Spring Sandwort, also known as Leadwort.

Leadwort is so called as it is found where there is a high lead content in the soil and can survive in these toxic conditions. Romans and miners used to use it to detect a good site to sink a mine and look for lead ore.

■ Peak District Mines Historical Society Ltd, Peak District Mining Museum, Matlock Bath, Derbyshire, DE4 3NR Tel:(01629) 583834

Sheldon Village

This village by Magpie Mine is set high on the hills overlooking the River Wye.

For hundreds of years it was the home of lead miners. The present church is dedicated to Saint Michael and All Angels and dates from 1865. Inside there are impressive timbers in the high steep angled roof.

The original oil lamps are now electrified . In the churchyard is a gravestone for a man named Ephraim Brocklehurst, who was killed at the Magpie Mine in January 1869 aged 25

Building of the present Sheldon village was from the time when lead mining was enjoying a prosperous period.

Chimney style

Another view of the Cornish Engine House, and the circular Cornish style chimney built in 1840 by Cornish miners who came with John Taylor.

Square chimneys (in the box right) are typical of the Derbyshire style built by the local miners

Haddon Hall

This beautiful and atmospheric residence is on a limestone outcrop overlooking the River Wye, near Bakewell and is the favourite of many a film director because of its unspoilt beauty...

This lovely medieval and Tudor manor house was once a sleeping beauty, unoccupied and falling into disrepair for 200 years, until brought to life with a kiss of restoration from the 9th Duke of Rutland when he moved here in the 1920s.

An old habitat

When the Domesday survey of 1087 was written, the dwelling then at Haddon was built and owned by William Peverel, thought to be the illegitimate son of William the conqueror. Little of this dwelling survives today.

The property passed though the decades to tenant William Avenel (1153), then the Vernon family (1170) and then later to the Manners family. Emblems of the Vernon and Manners families can be seen all over the hall. The peacock is a symbol of the Manners family and the Boar's head is a symbol of the Vernon family.

Almost a time capsule

The hall that Richard Vernon (William Avenel's son-in-law) inherited was smaller than the Haddon Hall we see today. All that survives from the place he would know are the Eagle Tower and the chapel. The family would have lived in the tower.

In 1195, a 12 foot wall was built around the hall. A lot of this wall is still standing. Crenellations, that now give the hall a distinctive skyline silhouette, were added later as a decorative feature.

In 1370 a lot of expansion work was carried out by another Vernon, also called Richard. He added the central banqueting hall, kitchens and parlour.

Haddon Hall has remained largely unchanged over the centuries and so is very popular with makers of period drama. Franco Zefferelli's Jane Eyre (1996) used Haddon Hall as Mr Rochester's house, Thornfield and The Princess Bride turned the hall into a royal palace. The BBC production of The Prince and the Pauper and Elizabeth with Cate Blanchett also used Haddon.

The film of Pride and Prejudice, starring Keira Knightley, changed Haddon's panelled banqueting hall into the inn at Lambton and the dining room became Elizabeth's bedroom.

The porch entrance from the courtyard of Haddon Hall

The exterior

The hall lies along the hillside like a battlemented fairytale castle, To reach it you have to cross a bridge of 1663. Entry to the interior of the hall is through the North-West Gate tower. The Vernon coat of arms can be seen above the top window.

In the courtyard is the lovely main arched doorway, with gargoyles peering down on visitors. This is in the central core of the medieval house, with its porch being added at a later date, probably about 1450. The octagonal bell tower in the right hand corner of the courtyard was added around then too, by Sir William Vernon. There are also more modern lead drainpipes with the symbols of the Vernon and Manners families on them. The lower courtyard also has an entrance into a small but fascinating museum where objects found at the hall from its previous occupants are displayed.

The entrance in the core of the medieval hall. The porch was added at a later date

Topiary of the two principal families of Haddon Hall can be seen as you enter the grounds, The Peacock is for the Manners family and the boar's head for the Vernon family

Below are gargoyles seen near the entrance porch

The lower courtyard is a good place to see the building style and additions of Haddon Hall over the years. Above are 'squinches' which link the different stages of building and also look very interesting as a feature

The battlemented roofline of the hall

A lead drainpipe section (above)

The North-West Gate Tower, added by Sir Henry Vernon (1445-1515). This is the main entrance

A strange carving

As you walk up to the entrance of the hall there is an Elizabethan stable block, above which is the restaurant and tea room.

Just through the archway into the stableblock, on the opposite wall, is a strange carving, though it was probably moved here from a different location, once over the main stable door. These images are usually found on churches.

It looks like an image known as a sheela-na-gig. This is an image of a woman in an indecorous pose, with legs open or around her head. Some people think it is a fertility symbol or a representation of the Earth Mother or goddess. The original meaning is now unknown.

The stables were converted into a kitchen in the early 20th century by the 9th duke. He had a tunnel built from there to the hall.

The chapel

The chapel at Haddon Hall, in the parish of Nether Haddon, is one of the smallest in the country. It is dedicated to St. Nicholas and has something from all stages in Haddon Hall's development. The oldest part is the south aisle, which faces you as you enter. The north aisle was added in the 14th century and the chancel in the 15th century. The pillars and the arches of the nave are Norman, as is the circular font. The box pews date from the 16th century. In the windows are examples of 15th century stained glass.

There are some wonderful wall paintings dating back to the 14th and 15th centuries to be seen in this tiny but perfectly formed place of worship. Once they would have been much more colourful. They survived in their faded but still beautiful form after being covered in whitewashed during the Reformation of the 16th century when such things were frowned upon. They were not rediscovered until the 1920s, when Haddon Hall was being restored. They include scenes from the life of St Nicholas, skeletons and floral jungle-like scenes (pictured right)

There is an emotive marble effigy of a young boy in the chapel. It is of Lord Haddon, the eldest son of the 8th Duke of Rutland who died in 1894. It is made more poignant by the fact that it was carved by his grieving mother. The one seen here is a copy made for the Haddon chapel, the original is at Belvoir Castle.

The circular Norman font, with wooden cover

Another font, with a carved head, to be seen in the chapel

Some of the rooms at Haddon Hall

On the right as you go in is the main and largest room, the Banqueting Hall, which dates from the late 14th century. This is the place that would have been the hub of life and main dwelling space in the medieval manor. Around 40 or 50 people would be bustling here day and night.

The minstrel's gallery was added about 1600. There is a 15th century refectory table in the room. It is on a raised dias creating an elevated position for the gentry. The top of the table is separate from the legs, so it could be turned over to show a clean side during the day when they were not eating. This is where the expression 'the tables have turned' comes from. Behind it is a tapestry reputed to have been given to the family by Henry VIII.

The roof is from the 20th century and was the major project for the 9th Duke. Oak timbers for it were cut from the Haddon or Belvoir estates.

The large fireplace was added about 100 years after the hall was built. Originally the fire would have been in the centre of the room.

The Kitchen

The kitchen is a preserved 14th century one and remains so unchanged it is easy to imagine the hustle and bustle of cooks preparing a banquet then. Wooden tables show the wear of centuries of busy hands chopping and working. Next to the kitchen is a bakery and a room containing 'dole' cupboards. They would have been left outside the hall for village people to take scraps of food or 'dole'. An example of a dole cupboard is pictured above.

The Dining Room

This used to be a high ceilinged medieval parlour, but the present height was formed by Sir Henry Vernon adding a lower ceiling in 1500. There are insignia from the families in the wooden carvings around the wall panels and the paintings in the ceiling design, as well as those of the royal family.

The Great Chamber

Once the upper half of the medieval parlour, it is decorated with tapestries and contains 17th century plasterwork and panelling. The panelling would once have been painted and there are traces of green and gold paint on the wood in places.

Carvings and glass from the Dining Room

The Long Gallery

This is the grandest room and is where people could parade up and down to get exercise without even venturing out of the house. There are large windows to maximise daylight. The diamond panels within the windows are deliberately set at angles to make them seem to sparkle in the light.

The ornate panelling and a grand door show again the family symbols. There are also images of roses and thistles entwined, dating from around 1603, which represent the union of England and Scotland. Above the fireplace is a painting of the hall by Rex Whistler (1933).

Steps leading up to the gallery from the banqueting hall

Elaborate Long Gallery door with Manners family peacock and windows from the Long Gallery

The Ante-Room and State Bedroom

After the Long Gallery is the ante room for the state bedroom. In here is a tapestry called 'Smelling'. The other senses from this tapestry collection are in other parts of the hall, Hearing Tasting and Feeling are on the landing and Seeing is above the Minstrel's Gallery.

In the State Bedroom there is an ornate plaster relief above the fireplace. It is a scene of Orpheus charming the beasts and has many creatures crammed within it. A peacock is shown larger than life – to remind us of the Manners family again. Some of the animals are quirky as maybe the artist had never seen some of them in the flesh so used imagination. This adds to the character of the piece, which probably dates from the mid 16th century.

Bear and elephant from the plaster relief above the State Bedroom fireplace

A romantic elopement

The last of the Vernon family to own Haddon Hall was Sir George Vernon. He had two daughters and no sons. Sir George, according to Camden was known as 'The King of the Peak'.

The somewhat romanticised tale that has come to be told is that he did not want his hall to be passed into the family of just anyone by the marriage of his daughters, so he was pretty picky about their suitors. He did not much like the suitor of his daughter Dorothy, John Manners, even though he was the son of the Earl of Rutland. He forbid Dorothy to see John again. John was not put off so easily and is said to have hidden in the woods nearby dressed as a woodsman to meet Dorothy in secret.

The story goes that at the wedding party, in 1563, of George's eldest daughter Margaret, (to Sir Thomas Stanley), Dorothy took her chance to elope and be with her John for good. The party was in full swing in the Long Gallery. With this distraction, Dorothy sneaked out of the back door into the garden and fled to her lover waiting by the small packhorse bridge over the River Wye. They rode through the night to Aylestone in Leicestershire where they were married.

This is a very romantic and possibly embroidered account of the story, which has all the appeal of Hollywood. Even as far back as the 1920s the story was well known. A film called Dorothy Vernon of Haddon Hall, starring Mary Pickford, was made then. John Manners was probably quite a good catch really.

The door through which Dorothy supposedly fled and the pack-horse bridge where John waited now both bear her name.

The pack-horse bridge now named after the lovestruck Dorothy

The gardens

The romantic gardens are mainly the work of the 9th Duchess of Rutland, at the beginning of the 20th century. The garden when she arrived was overgrown and unloved. Now there are glorious rose terraced gardens and lovely borders. From the gardens can be seen huge stone buttresses that hold up the outer walls of the hall and lovely views over Dorothy's bridge and the countryside..

There are many lovely flowers in the gardens, but in spring you may spot Fritillaries (left) in the grounds too

Saved by neglect

When Dorothy's father died in 1567, the hall passed to Dorothy and her husband John.

John Manners altered the Long Gallery to how it looks today. Later Dorothy's son George inherited, and then George's son, also named John. This John became the Earl of Rutland in 1641 and his home and focus moved to Belvoir. The old home of Haddon Hall was neglected and derelict through the 18th and 19th centuries. Ivy closed in on its walls and it became an almost forgotten treasure. Only a casual eye was kept on it by the family to make sure it was not totally falling down.

It was only when the Marquis of Granby, who became the 9th Duke of Rutland, decided to rediscover and restore Haddon Hall that it was once more loved and lived in. The fact that the hall had been left alone and unaltered during what was a time of major change of fashion in architecture and style, means that it escaped any major changes itself.

Haddon Hall is now the home of Lord Edward Manners and his wife. For further details contact: The Estate Office, Haddon Hall, Bakewell, Derbyshire DE45 1LA Telephone: (01629) 812855 email: info@haddonhall.co.uk   Website: www.haddonhall.co.uk

Hathersage

Did Robin Hood's trusted companion Little John get buried here? No one knows for sure, but what is certain is the lovely scenery, as well as a fine church and literary connections...

Now as we wander this pretty place it is hard to imagine it was once a dirty mill town producing the points on needles, the dust of which would damage many a lung.

Robin Hood connections

Hathersage is well known for its connections with the famous outlaw Robin Hood, he of the green tights and superb bowmanship. The truth about this character and where he was from is long debated. One school of thought has him coming from Loxley, which is not too far from Hathersage. That could give a believable connection between him and this village. Many places in the area have names connected with Robin Hood, including Hood Brook in the village and Robin Hood's Cave, up on Stanage Edge, which overlooks Hathersage.

Robin's right hand man Little John is said to be buried in the churchyard of St.Michael's and All Angels at Hathersage and for many years a large bow with arrows and a green cap were to be seen in the parish church, though no longer. One of the local pubs is now called The Little John Hotel to remind us of the village that is said to be his final resting place.

One of the hostelries in Hathersage, called after the famous character

A long worn road

Hathersage has long been a place many chose to rest in as they made the lonely way over the moors. It is mentioned in the census record the Domesday book of 1086. The name is then written 'Hereseige'.

Coming into Hathersage today from the Sheffield direction takes you over the brow of a hill and gives a sudden and wonderful vista, aptly called the Surprise View.

The stone from the edges around Hathersage were used to cut and form grindstones for the cutlery industry and pairs of millstones for grinding wheat, corn etc.

Packhorse trains brought metal from Sheffield to be used in the button and needle mills once thriving in the village and brought millstones, salt pottery and lead ore along the road too, which became so busy a turnpike road was built with a toll house to collect fees for using it.

Now people coming to enjoy Hathersage walk, drive, catch buses or arrive by rail, as the village is on the main Sheffield-Manchester line.

This 1914 street lamp can be seen opposite the Little John Hotel

The Surprise View on the Hathersage-Sheffield Road

45

Hathersage parish church

If Little John is indeed buried here, or if he even existed except in myth along with Robin, he chose a lovely spot. What is said to be his grave is 3.5 metres long.

Little John was so called as a joke, as he was described as very tall. His supposed grave was opened in 1784 and in it a large thigh bone was said to have been found. If so it was of a size to be that of a very tall man, about 7ft tall... but the bone is not available for verfication.

Another less romantic explanation is that two posts or stones that were once all that marked the area now called a grave, were in fact used as a standard unit of length. This unit was called a 'perch.' Each village had its own measure, so it would be a standard length when selling or buying.

A novel way of collecting donations from people visiting Little John's grave is in the form of an old parking meter! (right)

HERE LIES BURIED
LITTLE JOHN
THE FRIEND & LIEUTENANT OF
ROBIN HOOD –
HE DIED IN A COTTAGE (NOW DESTROYED)
TO THE EAST OF THE CHURCHYARD
THE GRAVE IS MARKED BY
THIS OLD HEADSTONE & FOOTSTONE
AND IS UNDERNEATH THIS OLD YEW TREE

DRY WEATHER FOOTPATH TO THE CHURCH

PUBLIC FOOTPATH TO THE CHURCH
200 mts..on the right.

The remains of the Saxon Cross

The church is dedicated to St. Michael and All Angels. It is not mentioned in the Domesday Book but there has long been a site of preaching or worship here. The present church would have been built on the site of earlier worship. Parts of the building there today date from the mid 14th century.

The Saxon cross, still in the churchyard, would have been used as a point to preach from before a church was built. The Eyre family, well known locally, were responsible for a lot of changes and building work on the church that came later. As with many churches, St Michael's was much restored in the Victorian era, with a lot of the original layout being altered, including the roof and chancel floor being highered.

It was in the church vicarage that the novelist Charlotte Bronte stayed when she visited the village. Her friend's brother, Frank Nussey, was the vicar of St Michael's.

Camp Green

This earthwork near the church is circular and surrounded by a ditch. It is an trace of an early settlement in Hathersage, and is thought to be Norman.

The lychgate

The entrance into the churchyard is graced by a pretty roofed gateway called a lychgate, shown bottom right. This is where the vicar or mourners could take a seat to wait for the hearse and coffin to arrive, or get it up on their shoulders. There is a tudor rose emblem carved on it.

Look out for gargoyles above you

Inside the church

The hexagonal font dates from around 1440 and has shields of local families, including the Eyre and Padley family, on it as decoration.

The west window is dedicated to the memory of William and Mary Eyre of nearby North Lees Hall.

It was unveiled in 1856 and restored in 2001.

There are two rather ornately carved chairs to be seen, too. These are said in the church guide book to have been used by Queen Victoria and Albert when they opened the St George's Hall in Liverpool.

The chairs were given to the church, as stone for the hall was quarried from this district.

The stone face pictured right can be seen on the wall near the chairs.

One of the angels carved in the roof

A stone arch in the church, beneath which are the brasses of Robert Eyre, who died in 1459, and his wife Joan. Four sons kneel beside their father

Right: An angel from one of the windows

A face on a pillar of the sedilia. A sedilia is a stone seat for the clergy to use

A view from the churchyard

47

Life at the sharp end

Originally a small agricultural village, Hathersage joined in the industrial growth of the country in the 17th and 18th centuries. In the 17th century there was a lead smelting industry around Hathersage, which used coal fired furnaces called 'cupolas'. Several small mills were opened, to make buttons and then later wire, needles and pins. There was also once a paper mill which provided wrapping for the products. The air would then have been full of smoke from the mills.

It was not only smoke that would have been bad for health. Needlemaking was a job which produced metal dust as grindstones were used to sharpen the points, a dangerous stuff to lodge in the lungs of many an unfortunate worker. A 19th century investigation into the bad working conditions led to some improvements.

One of the mills was owned by a man callled Robert Cook, who made needles at Barnfield Mill, which was built in 1811 and used the stream to provide power for the machines.

Another mill a little further along Mill Lane is Victoria Mill, which was built in 1820 and was run by a family named Child.

Dale Mill was powered by water from Dale Brook and was where brass buttons were made as early as 1720. Later it was converted to use steam power and needles were produced there.

Samuel Fox, attributed with inventing the steel ribbed umbrella frame, (see page 24) once also worked at Hathersage, for the Cocker family, who set up the Dale Mill.

By the turn of the century the major businesses had transferred to Sheffield or closed altogether.

This advertisement was in the White's Sheffield Directory for 1868 (P247)

TOBIAS CHILD & CO.
MANUFACTURERS OF
Hackle, Gill, & all kinds of Flat Pins,
GILLS, HAND & MACHINE HACKLES
FOR FLAX, WOOL, COTTON, SILK, AND TOW;
Improved Wood Card Covering, &c.
CAST STEEL WIRE DRAWERS & REFINERS,
SPIRAL SPRINGS, LOOM SPRINGS,
DEALERS IN FILES & STEEL, & GENERAL MERCHANTS.
VICTORIA WORKS, HATHERSAGE,
NEAR SHEFFIELD.   247

Old cottages

On Besom Lane is a row of cottages with a row of smaller windows at the top. The top floor was a button factory, A besom is a broom made from twigs, like a broomstick

Some of the views as you walk down Mill Lane

Some street names seem to reflect old use or local trade – according to the Shorter Oxford English Dictionary a 'baulk' is made in ploughing when ridges are left and 'cog' is to wheedle or quibble – perhaps over goods on packhorse trains

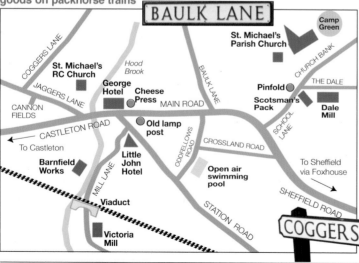

The George Hotel

This hotel was built around the 1500s as an inn for travellers and would have served the packhorse trains that wound their way from Castleton and Sheffield.

When Charlotte Bronte visited the village the landlord of the inn was called Morton. She used this as the name for the village in Jane Eyre, which she based on Hathersage. Charlotte arrived at The George by stagecoach when she came to visit.

■ The George Hotel. Hathersage, Derbyshire, S32 1BB ■ Telephone: (01433) 650436
■ www.george-hotel.net

The George Hotel and a stained glass window of St. George there

At the bottom of Church Bank is a 1660 pinfold for holding stray animals

Near the George Hotel stands this old cheese press (above). The weight would squeeze out the watery whey from the curds and turn it into cheese.

The Roman Catholic Church

A Catholic chapel was built on this site in 1692, but it was destroyed inside by Cromwell, leaving just the walls standing. Later, Thomas Eyre of Hassop left money in his will for a new chapel, with which the old chapel was restored and reopened in 1806, with a priest's house built beside it.

The Scotsman's Pack

The name of this inn in the village could well come from the travelling tradesmen using the old routes. They were called 'scotsmen' because of the packs of Scottish linen they sold and would have been a familiar sight passing through the village.

The swimming pool

Hathersage has a heated outdoor swimming pool, with a cafe and play area. The pool was opened in 1936 but was then unheated, with water being pumped from the village brook.

■ Oddfellows Road, Hathersage, Hope Valley, S32 1BU
■ Telephone: (01433) 650843 (Cafe, 01433 651159)

A pretty hostelry

If you carry on down Mill Lane from Hathersage, the path leads to Leadmill Bridge. On Grindleford Road by the Leadmill Bridge is a picturesque old 16th century inn, called The Plough. It is now a good eating place too.

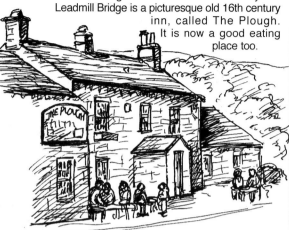

Stanage Edge

This impressive natural feature overlooks Hathersage and is a magnet for climbers, who swarm along the huge rockface like brightly clad ants.

The edge can be reached by a minor road that leads up by Hood Brook from Hathersage. It is a wonderful place strewn with huge boulders and the views are tremendous. It has been used as a film set many times, for example in The Princess Bride and Jane Eyre.

Robin Hood's Cave on Stanage Edge is a cosy little place for a rest. With a little imagination you can imagine him sitting here sharpening his arrows!

The packhorse trains carrying all sorts of goods to and from towns would have wound their way from Hathersage up to

Stanage Edge and on towards Sheffield along a paved track called the 'long causeway'. This track can still be seen near Stanedge Pole (the difference in spelling can be confusing). The pole was set there as a marker to let people know they were on the correct route.

Other well worn ways can be seen in the Peak, including a hollowed out track from the Surprise View leading down the moor towards Burbage Brook. Millstones would also have been taken along these tracks.

In Hathersage village, one of the road names, Jaggers Lane, is a reminder of the packhorse trains. The leader of the train was called a 'jagger.'

Track along the top of Stanage Edge. The drawing shows Stanedge Pole

Another view of
Stanage Edge and
the hills beyond

The Bronte Connection

The novelist Charlotte Bronte, who created Jane Eyre, one of the great romantic literary heroines, was a visitor to Hathersage. She stayed with her friend Ellen Nussey in 1845, at the vicarage. She wrote Jane Eyre in 1847, and the visit seems to have been a great inspiration for her.

Ellen's brother was the vicar of Hathersage between 1844 and 1847. It is said he once proposed to Charlotte and asked her to work in the school. This could have given her the idea for St John Rivers proposing to Jane Eyre in the story.

Charlotte also mentions the needle mills. The area described by Charlotte fits the Peaks and Hathersage well, but she changed the name of the village, thought to be based on Hathersage, to Morton.

North Lees Hall

This romantic Elizabethan property stands about two miles to the north of Hathersage. There has been a property on the site since medieval times

The current hall was built in the early 1590s for William Jessop, by the Elizabethan architect Robert Smythson, who was also responsible for Hardwick Hall. Inside it is richly decorated with plasterwork friezes.

The most well known tenants were the Eyres. Members of this influential local family were living in the house when Charlotte came to the area and she and her friend Ellen visited them.

The hall is now thought to be immortalised in her famous story, as North Lees Hall is widely accepted to have been the place called Thornfield, Mr Rochester's house, in the novel. Indeed it looks every inch the same as the Thornfield described:

"three storeys high, of proportions not vast, though considerable; a gentleman's manor house, not a noblemans seat; battlements around the top gave it a picturesque look."

The name too seems to have been conjured up from North Lees Hall. 'Thorn' is an anagram of 'north' and 'lees' means 'pasture or field.' Also Charlotte describes the Apostle's Cabinet, which is a piece of furniture unique to North Lees Hall.

As in the novel, there is a tale of a 'mad' woman in the history of North Lees Hall that may have inspired Charlotte. The first mistress of the hall is reputed to have become demented and confined to a room on the second floor. She too met her end in a fire.

By 1959 North Lees Hall was in a ruinous condition. The owner then was one Sir Hugh Beach and he gave the job of restoring the place to an architect called Gerald Haythornthwaite.

Work was completed in 1964 and it was used as a guest house. The estate was bought by the Peak Park Joint Planning Board in 1971.

In 1987 they approached the Vivat Trust, (a non profit making preservation trust that secures buildings of historical, architectural or industrial interest), to manage North Lees Hall.

The hall re-opened in 1989. It has recently undergone renovation and is available to rent as a holiday property.

■ The Vivat Trust offer holidays in their properties nationwide, including North Lees Hall.
■ www.vivat.org.uk
■ Telephone: 0845 090 0194
■ e mail: enquiries@vivat.org.uk)

Dry stone walls

Dry stone walls are a defining feature of Derbyshire and the Peak District. like old bones peeking through green muscles. Using the rocks to create a boundary or enclosure is an ancient craft and takes a lot of skill...

D ry stone walls do not contain any mortar, but are held together because of the way in which the stones are placed. Different parts of the country have different styles of dry stone walls. Many stand on much earlier boundaries.

General method

The walls are usually a rough 'A' in cross-section. They widen towards the bottom to give a more stable construction and larger stones are placed at the bottom for stability too.

'Through' stones are placed half way up the wall. These are bigger and, as the name suggests, go all the way through the structure, to tie it together.

The middle of the wall is filled with rubble to pack and strengthen it. Along the top are placed smaller, vertical stones, that are usually cut or dressed into a triangular or semi-circular shape. These are called cope stones.

Walls made of both limestone and grit stone can be seen in the Peak District. The limestone rocks have many fossils in them, of animals and plants trapped when the rocks were formed millions of years ago.

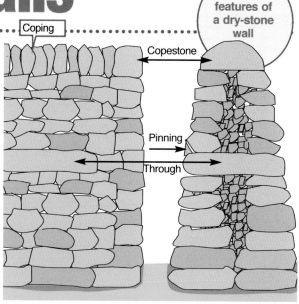

General features of a dry-stone wall

Coping

Copestone

Pinning

Through

Wildlife and flora

Dry stone walls also provide a home for many small animals. birds and insects. Frogs, newts and snails like the bottom of the walls where it is moist and field mice often use the middle of the walls to make a nest in. Insects like the little nooks and crannies to hide in.

Lichen

Moss, ivy, ferns and lichen also grow on the walls. Moss grows on the north side mostly, as this is in sun less and more moist.

Lichen is not a single organism but a combination of two living symbiotically (both exist together with mutual benefit to each other). Most of the lichen is made of a a fungus but in the fungus there are also algal cells, meaning that the lichen is a mix of both fungus and alga. The idea that lichen was a symbiotic relationship of these two organisms was first championed in this country by Beatrix Potter, famous for her illustrated children's books. She also did many paintings of lichens.

■ For more information on dry stone walls or how to become a Stone Waller, contact the National Stone Centre, Porter Lane, Middleton by Wirksworth, Derbyshire DE4 4LS

■ Tel: (01629) 824833 ■ www.nationalstonecentre.org.uk

Holes left in walls for animals to get through are called 'smoots'

Hardwick Hall

A woman to be reckoned with, Bess of Hardwick is remembered in the grand halls she built. Her residence at Hardwick is a tribute to her vision and wealth and still impresses today...

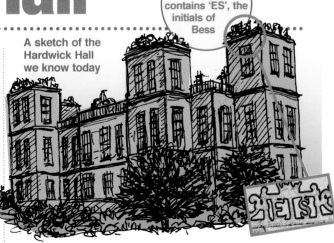

A sketch of the Hardwick Hall we know today

The edifice of Hardwick Hall contains 'ES', the initials of Bess

Bess of Hardwick was a businesswoman, ambitious herself and also the partner of four wealthy, succesful husbands.

A strong woman

Elizabeth, Countess of Shrewsbury, began life at Hardwick in 1527, born into a family of four girls and a boy. The family had lived at Hardwick for at least six generations and were minor gentry, owning land and living in a small manor house on the site of Hardwick Old Hall. The name Hardwick means 'sheep-farm.

The year after she was born, Bess's father died. Bess took the route of many children of Tudor gentry and became a 'gentle-woman' or 'upper servant' in the house of a neighbouring wealthy family. This was seen as a good way to be educated into society and become more marriageworthy. It seems to have worked well, as in 1543 Bess married her cousin, Robert Barlow, a wealthy young man, though he died just a few months after their wedding. Bess was left with an income of around £66 a year and would probably have carried on working for families as before. She was obviously still out in the world socialising as she was married again four years later, to Sir William Cavendish.

William was much wealthier than Bess and the match increased her social status. He was also a government servant and older than Bess. He owned a lot of property, but sold it and bought some in Derbyshire. He certainly had a lot of cash and an eye for the grand, as among his purchases was the house and estate of Chatsworth, which he bought in 1549. It was not the Chatsworth house we see today, but one that he had built after pulling down an older one on the site.

The marriage produced eight children, but two died in infancy, before William died in 1557. Bess was left with an interest in Chatsworth and a lot more property too. No doubt this made her an even more attractive marriage prospect, as well as her noted vitality and beauty and it was only two years before matrimony beckoned again. This time it was to a West Country landowner called Sir William St. Loe and took Bess even further up the rungs of respectability as he was a butler in the Royal Household and a favourite courtier of the Queen. The couple were only together five years before he died in 1564. He too left most of his property to Bess.

A fourth and final husband

Her fourth and last husband was also a great catch for Bess. He was George Talbot, the 6th Earl of Shrewsbury, a 40 year old widower and head of one of England's richest families. They wed in 1567. He has another claim to fame too, as the keeper of that famous and unfortunate royal, Mary Queen of Scots. Just two years after he married Bess, he was given the task of looking after the 'captive queen' and he did so until 1584.

Mary was moved between many of his properties, including Sheffield Castle, Sheffield Manor, Wingfield Manor and Bess's house at Chatsworth. She never stayed at Hardwick Hall, even though a room there is named after her.

The Cavendish crest, a knotted snake, can be seen on many places around the hall, including the lead gutters around the entrance. The family motto was *'Cavendo Tutus'* **(Safe by being on guard)**

Rocky relations

Looking after Mary was a great strain on the marriage. Another problem was that Bess, in 1574, had married off her daughter Elizabeth to Charles Stuart, the brother of Mary's ex-husband Lord Darnley. A child of this marriage had a claim to the throne and more than likely Bess had this in mind when she got them together. Queen Elizabeth was not happy about the marriage and neither was Bess's husband.

Elizabeth and Charles both died within a few years and Bess was left as guardian of their daughter Arabella Stuart.

Another thing to annoy the seemingly long-suffering George was that Bess was rebuilding her house at Chatsworth and spending lots of her time and his money on it.

A gryphon from the fireplace in the High Great Chamber

The couple split in 1583 and argued for many years about who should have Chatsworth. Bess took the house that was not in dispute to live in – that at Hardwick. Bess decided to improve the place and between 1585 and 1590 she replaced the house there with what is now called Hardwick Old Hall.

When Lord Shrewsbury died, in 1590, she got control of all the lands again and was one of the richest people in England. He was buried in a grand tomb that is found at the right hand side of the Shrewsbury Chapel in Sheffield Anglican Cathedral. Even though his widow Bess had just finished one hall, she began using some of her fortune to plan another, much grander house just next to it. She never really used Chatsworth much after all the earlier arguments. Maybe it held too many bad feelings. Bess spent the next thirteen years building designing and furnishing the new Hardwick Hall as well as trying to control her granddaughter Arabella.

Arabella seems to have been wayward and difficult person to keep in check and as ambitious as her grandmother. Unfortunately her life did not work out well. After many intruiges and a marriage to The Earl of Hereford, who was also a claimant to the throne and so unpopular with the Queen, she ended up in the Tower of London and died there in 1615.

Mary Queen of Scots

Bess died in 1608. One of the legends that has come to be told is that she was told she would never die whilst she was building, and that is why she kept on doing so.

She is buried in All Hallowes, what is now the cathedral, at Derby.

A grand residence - mark two

The Hardwick Hall of today is the second one built by Bess. The first one, now the impressive ruin called Hardwick Old Hall, is just next to it. Both halls were more or less furnished and in use at the same time, which reflects how rich they were being able to support two such grand homes.

Bess continued to live in the Old Hall until the new, second one was finished in 1597. Later the old hall was used to provide extra guest rooms and servant's quarters.

As the new hall was a brand new building, and not an expansion or adaption of an older building, it is very well designed and proportioned, with great symmetry. It is most likely that the plans were by a well known Elizabethan architect and master stonemason called Robert Smythson.

As well as having the cash, Bess was in a good position to provide the raw materials for her new project. Stone for the hall came from a quarry down the hill, timber from her own woods and glass most likely from her glassworks at Wingfield. As the now familiar phrase 'Hardwick Hall, more glass than wall' implies, the windows are much larger than was usual and set a new precedent. Glass was very expensive at the time and using so much of it was a great status symbol.

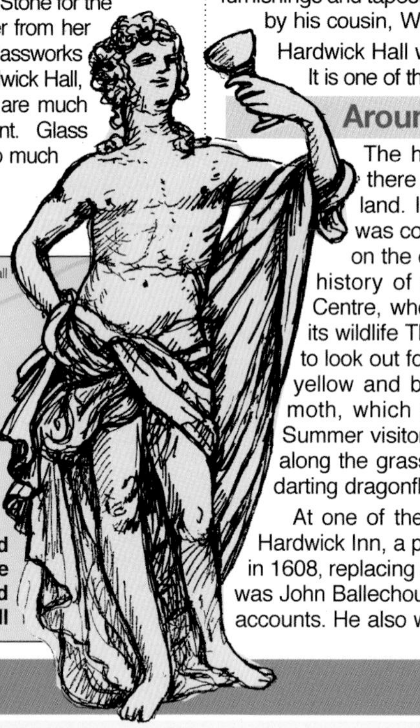

■ Hardwick Hall is now in the care of The National Trust

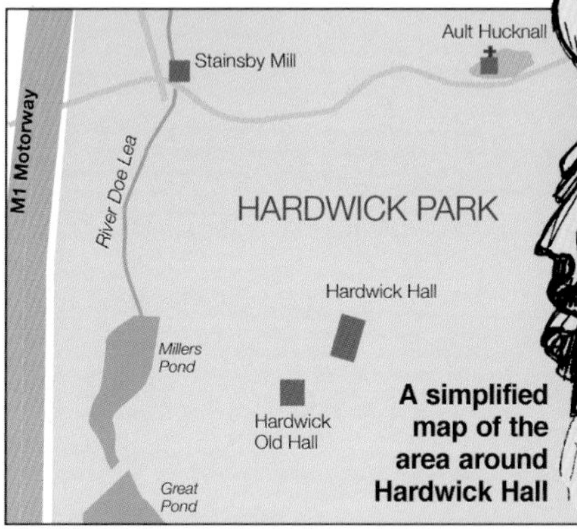

When Bess died, her second son, William, took over the halls at Hardwick and he also inherited Chatsworth when his older brother died in 1616. In 1618 he was created Earl of Devonshire. William spend more time at Hardwick and made many improvements before he died in 1626. His son inherited the properties but only survived his father by two years, dying in 1628 at the age of 38. This Earl was the one who employed the philosopher and author Thomas Hobbes.

One of the more colourful characters in the hall's history is the 6th Duke, who was also known as 'The Bachelor Duke'. He inherited Hardwick in 1811 when he was 21 and was an extravagant sort of fellow who spent lots of money putting more furnishings and tapestries in. He died in 1858 and was succeeded by his cousin, William Cavendish, as 7th Duke.

Hardwick Hall was acquired by the National Trust in 1959. It is one of the must-sees of great country houses.

Around the exterior

The hall has lovely gardens and orchards and there are around 1000 acres of park and woodland. In the 1970s, the western part of the park was converted into a Country Park. There is also on the estate The Stone Centre, which tells of the history of stone and stonemasons and The Park Centre, where you can learn about the parkland and its wildlife There are many sorts of wildlife and flowers to look out for. You may spot peacock butterflies, or the yellow and black banded caterpillars of the cinnabar moth, which feed on the (poisonous) ragwort plant. Summer visitors are the soaring swallows, sweeping low along the grass. The ponds are home to water vole and darting dragonflies.

At one of the Southern entrances to Hardwick is the Hardwick Inn, a pretty and popular public house. It was built in 1608, replacing an earlier inn on the same site. The builder was John Ballechouse, also known as John Painter in the hall accounts. He also worked on building the new hall for Bess.

Peacock butterfly and cinnabar moth caterpillars on ragwort

A simplified map of the area around Hardwick Hall

(Map labels: M1 Motorway, River Doe Lea, Stainsby Mill, Ault Hucknall, HARDWICK PARK, Hardwick Hall, Millers Pond, Hardwick Old Hall, Great Pond)

Inside the hall

The most impressive room inside Hardwick Hall is the High Great Chamber. This room by Bess's time had taken over the same role as the Great Hall of Medieval times and was where guests were received and entertained It was the place for singing, dancing and plays, as well as where meals were served. The food would have been brought to the tables with a formal procession all the way from the kitchen and would have been a grand affair and also possibly rather cold!.

The decoration is superb, with a wonderful frieze and an elaborate fireplace surround which includes the royal coat of arms. Bess had always the hope of joining the royal family and enjoyed a chance to display loyalty to the Queen. Some of the original paint that would have coloured the chamber's frieze can still be seen, though it would once have been more bright in hue.

The theme of the frieze is the forest, with the court of the goddess Diana. There are a delightful selection of animals to spot, including deer, lions, elephants, monkeys, boars and camels.

There are many other impressive rooms to see as you take the tour around this magnificent and grand home, including the Long Gallery, where people would have strolled for their exercise in inclement weather, the Green Velvet Room with an 18th century bed, the Chapel and the Kitchens.

One room is called Mary Queen of Scot's Room, even though the hall was not built by the time the unfortunate monarch came to her end.

Many of the furnishings at Hardwick and in the room, however, would have been familiar to Mary as they were brought over from Chatsworth, where she did stay. Over the door in the room at Hardwick which bears her name is a semi circlular panel which has on it the royal coat of arms and her initials M R. This is most likely to have been brought from Mary's apartments at Chatsworth.

One of the other treats is an exhibition called The Threads of Time, which opened in 2005 and has many lovely previously unseen examples of embroidery and tapestry from Hardwick Hall on display, some by Bess herself.

Some of the designs to be seen in the Threads of Time exhibition

Coney was another name for rabbit in Elizabeth's time. These two are found on a tapestry at the top of the stairs near the High Great Chamber

■ For more details about Hardwick Hall contact: Hardwick Hall, Doe Lea, Chesterfield, Derbyshire S44 5QJ
■ Tel: (01246) 850430 ■ e-mail: hardwickhall@nationaltrust.org.uk ■ Website: www.nationaltrust.org.uk

Hardwick Old Hall

Hardwick Old Hall and some of the fine plasterwork there

This hall is where Bess of Hardwick decided to live after she had argued with and split from her husband, the Earl of Shrewsbury, in 1583.

The house on the site then was much different and Bess used her wealth to massively extend and improve the old Hardwick house into a grander hall. No doubt many of the things she planned and experienced whilst building what is now known as Hardwick Old Hall were very useful when she built her other and even grander Hardwick Hall next to it.

There are some fine examples of plasterwork surviving on what are now ruins of this once fine hall. In what is now called the Forest Great Chamber, there is a scene of deer, trees and shrubs. This was made by Abraham Smith, who had also worked for Bess at Chatsworth and is what gives this room its name. Deer are also Bess's emblems and the oak trees represent constancy. There is also a door in the scene.

Another scene is that of the biblical story of Tobias, which is on an overmantel in what used to be the nursery. The story of Tobias and the angel was a favourite one for Bess.

By the 18th century the Dukes of Devonshire began to live more at Chatsworth than at Hardwick and the Old Hall was partly demolished so parts of it could be reused or sold. It became a romantic ruin that was popular with artists and visitors.

In the 1990s the ruins were made safe and some repair and conservation work carried out. There are many nooks and crannies to discover wandering the ruins, with fireplaces, empty windows full of sky and a sense of centuries.

The Old Hall is now managed by English Heritage and there is a shop and information in what used to be the kitchen of the hall.

■ Tel: (01246) 850431
■ Website: www.english-heritage.org.uk

Stainsby Mill

This old grain mill is also on the Hardwick estate. A mill has stood on this site since as far back as the 13th century.

Until 1593 it was owned by the Savage family, Lords of the Manor of Stainsby, when it was bought by Bess of Hardwick. The mill would have supplied Hardwick's kitchens with flour as well as fodder for the animals. was designed so it could be operated by just one person.

By the mid 1800s the mill was in a derelict state, no longer used and so the 6th Duke of Devonshire decided to modernise it, with new equipment and rebuilding which was completed by 1850.

New owners, Kirkland and Son of Mansfield also added a new , larger waterwheel,

Over the years more improvement and modernisation was carried out, but by 1952 the mill was no longer in production.

The mill passed to the National Trust in 1976 and was extensively restored, opening to the public in 1992. Now once again, there is flour milled there on certain days.

Visitors can look around this fascinating little place that once produced best white flour for the upper classes and brown flour for the lower, with any waste left for the animals. And all using the power of water. Very eco-friendly!

■ Stainsby Mill: Tel: (01246) 850430 ■ e-mail: stainsbymill@nationaltrust,org.uk ■ Website: www.nationaltrust.org.uk

Ault Hucknall

This quiet spot has a lovely old church that holds some wonderful carvings and a philosopher's resting place

This tiny place which consists of just a fine old church, a farm and a handful of houses is perhaps one of the smallest villages in England, if not the smallest.

An ancient and sacred site

Ault Hucknall's church of St. John The Baptist is unfortunately sometimes locked, but the exterior alone is a gem.

It has been a place of worship for over a 1000 years. There are some fine Norman carvings and it is well worth a detour if you are at Stainsby Mill, which is about a mile away, or Hardwick Hall, which is less than two miles away. It is also only two miles from the M1, but you could be a world away in this quiet and ancient spot that has long provided a place of worship.

Though the name sounds like it could be a corruption of 'old' Hucknall, it is thought that the name comes from the French word *Hault,* which means high, as the village is indeed high up – Hucknall derives from the name of someone, Hucca.

The interior

There is a Norman chancel arch, two green men in the roof bosses and some interesting tombs if you are lucky enough to find the church open. There is also some mediaeval stained glass. One window, dating from 1528, is a memorial to Bess of Hardwick's father, John Hardwick.

The church also has a Cavendish Chapel. The only Cavendish tomb in there is that of Anne Keighley, the 1st Countess of Devonshire, which is made of alabaster and has carvings of figures representing the muses. Most of the Cavendish family were buried at Edensor, near Chatsworth, as was her husband.

Thomas Hobbes (1588-1679)

On the floor near Anne's tomb is a black marble slab marking the grave of the 16th century political philosopher and author Thomas Hobbes. He was tutor for two Earls of Devonshire, father and son.

Thomas Hobbes was born in Wiltshire, at Malmesbury in 1588, the year of the Spanish Armada. The tale goes that his mother gave birth to him prematurely due to the shock of hearing about this invasion by sea.

Hobbes later attended Oxford and was a controversial thinker and writer. His first book was about the wonders of the Peak District, but in 1651 he wrote his great work Leviathan, about the nature, purpose and justification of government.

He died at Hardwick Hall on December 4th 1679, aged 91 and was laid to rest at St. John The Baptist's.

Here be a dragon...

In the West wall is a blocked door with a Norman arch and tympanum. A tympanum is the semi-circular space above the lintel, which is usually highly decorated. Tympanum means 'drum.'

The tympanum (1)

The carving on the tympanum at Old Hucknall is worn, but shows what looks like a centaur (half human half horse) waving a palm in the right hand and a cross in the left. To the right is a figure or beast that seems to be falling back in awe or fear and maybe has clawed feet and wings.

There is seen bottom right what could be an Agnus Dei (Lamb of God) or another small animal. It looks a bit like a fox too.

It is also possible it represents the story of St. Margaret of Antioch emerging from the body of a devil or dragon: Margaret was the daughter of a pagan priest, but she became a Christian. The legend says that her father threw her out, but another pagan saw her and wanted to marry her. She refused him and also kept her faith and so he had her put in jail. Whilst captive she fought a dragon that almost swallowed her, but she escaped by scratching its throat with a cross she was carrying. She still came to a bad end – she was tortured and then beheaded.

The blocked door with the tympanum and lintel above

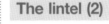

The lintel (2)

The lintel shows a man fighting a beast. It could be St. George and the Dragon, who are separated by a cross which is where the two pieces seem to have been joined. It could also represent St. Michael fighting with Satan. The fighting figure has a Norman shield and St George had not become England's patron saint by then. There is a loop shape on the left. Maybe this represents a plan of a Norman castle

There are interesting stones to be found in the church yard

A Norman window and fragment of carved stone can also be seen

The church is usually open 1pm - 5pm every Saturday during the summer until early October. A web site with more information can be found at www.tonybell.co.uk

Calver Bridge

Calver Bridge, given added character by moss and wildflowers

At this spot is a lovely old river bridge and a mill that was once a TV star. A walk along the river bank leads to the old weir that is usually inhabited by friendly ducks...

Calver is a lovely spot to potter, with a craft shop and tea rooms for a treat and a river to watch the wildlife and nod at the cows as you walk along its banks.

Lead connections

There are three areas to the area known as Calver: Calver Sough, Calver Bridge and Calver village itself. The sough gets its name from lead mining connections. A sough is an underground channel built to drain mine water away.

At the centre of Calver village is an old cross and there are several pubs, including the Eyre Arms and the Derwentwater Arms. The other main pub is the Bridge Inn, though this is technically in Curbar.

Once at Calver crossroads was a large footwear factory that made metal capped boots used by miners. It is now shop units and there is a garden centre behind it.

There is also the Derbyshire Craft Centre and Eating house, near the bridge to visit, as well as a small gallery.

The Bridge and Mill

The lovely 18th century bridge is the main focus at Calver Bridge as may be expected by the name. It arches over the River Derwent giving a lovely view along the rippling waters overhung by trees.

By the side of the river is a huge cotton mill, which once drew its power from the waters.

The mill first built on the site was destroyed by fire and rebuilt in 1804. It worked as a cotton mill until 1923. Now it has a new lease of life as riverside flats.

Once the mill had a brief taste of stardom when it was used as a stand in for the prisoner of war prison Colditz in the 1960s TV series of the same name. It must have been odd seeing the occasional Nazi officer chasing escapees around this quiet spot in the middle of the Peak District .

The Weir

Walking along the riverside from the mill along a path opposite the Bridge Inn, called Duke's Drive, you eventually come to Calver Weir. The weir was built about 1778 when John Pares and John Gardom built the cotton mill at Calver.

Calver weir showing damage before restoration

Floods swept it away the following year but it was rebuilt with a new goyt between 1799 and 1804.

In 1833 the weir and mill goyt were enlarged to drive two new waterwheels at the mill.

Kingfisher

The weir is now a Grade 2 listed structure and has recently undergone much needed repair and restoration by the Calver Weir Restoration Project. More about the project can be found on their website: www.calverweir.org.uk. Walking by the river you may spot Mallards, Coots, Moorhens, a Dipper, a bobbing Grey Wagtail or a blue darting Kingfisher. Maybe even a Water Vole scurrying. Plants to see include yellow loosestrife, Himalayan Balsam, Cow Parsley and Red Clover.

The pinfold

Up Pinfold Hill to the left of the church you come to the **pinfold** on the right. A sheep rounder-upper was called a pinder. There was a fine to release any livestock found wandering loose and put in it.

PINFOLD HILL

Dipper

This house is by the river just before the weir. In the foreground is Indian/Himalayan Balsam. Right: Red Clover and water vole

Stoney Middleton

This picturesque place has an unusually shaped church and observes the Derbyshire custom of welldressing, when brightly coloured pictures, made mainly of flowers, deck wells and springs...

Springs here were perhaps a reason why people began living in this spot and the area around the village church is believed to have been held sacred and used for worship since Celtic times.

A gift of water

Warmed water springing from the Earth is a pretty wonderful thing and our ancestors thought so too. They gave thanks for the water by dedicating the springs to a god or goddess.

The spring was used as a shrine, with perhaps a statue of the goddess there, or a stone head, like those connected with the Brigantes tribe. The people would leave offerings of flowers, coins etc. Many thought that the waters had healing properties, a belief which is still held today too, as those who brave the taste of spa waters at various places may find out or not! Also the custom of throwing coins into the water still persists today, as a glance into many public fountains or ponds will show.

The wells used by Druids and Pagan religions were later used by the Romans to worship their gods and goddesses and they too would worship leave offerings at the wells. Roman coins have been found in the area, perhaps after being cast into the well waters. These venerated wells became absorbed by the new culture and used by all for their various forms of worship, whether openly or not.

Again, when the new religion of Christianity was brought to the Peak District, the wells were absorbed and given into the care of the Christian Saint Martin.

Stoney Middleton at well dressing time, with the bunting up

'The Roman Baths'

The beautifully restored bath house

The building in Stoney Middleton, shown above, is popularly known as the 'Roman Baths', but there is no evidence found as yet to show there was ever a Roman Bath here. Roman coins have been found nearby though and the Romans would have probably known of any springs.

Others did bathe in the springs here, though, to partake in the waters that were believed to have curative properties. The waters are at a constant temperature of 63° F and were thought to help rheumatism, amongst other ailments.

In 1789, a writer called Pilkington made the suggestion that more people might bathe if the waters were more private or covered in. Early the next century this was carried out, by a man called Thomas Denman of Stoney Middleton Hall.

By 1815 there was a new 'Roman style' building with separate baths for men and women, with each having their own window, changing rooms and fireplace.

The expected spa boom did not occur though and the baths fell into disrepair.

In 1980, the building was 'listed' and between 1985 and 1992 were extensively restored to the fine condition they are in today.

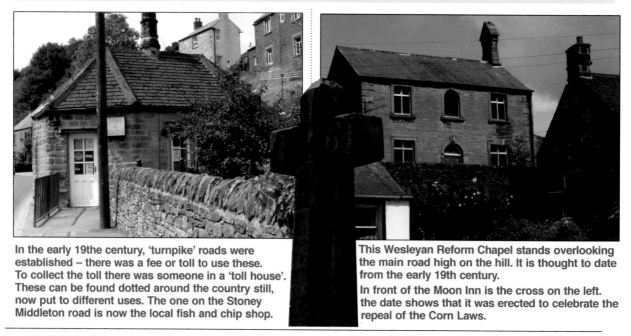

In the early 19the century, 'turnpike' roads were established – there was a fee or toll to use these. To collect the toll there was someone in a 'toll house'. These can be found dotted around the country still, now put to different uses. The one on the Stoney Middleton road is now the local fish and chip shop.

This Wesleyan Reform Chapel stands overlooking the main road high on the hill. It is thought to date from the early 19th century.

In front of the Moon Inn is the cross on the left. the date shows that it was erected to celebrate the repeal of the Corn Laws.

Saint Martin's Church

The wealthy local Eyre family are linked with the church at Stoney Middleton. Robert Eyre, of Highlow Hall, married Joan, heiress to the Manor of Padley and it says in local folklore that they met at the St Martin's well, as the springs were by then called. A wooden church was probably also on the site by then. The couple had a stone church built, said to be a symbol of their love and a thanksgiving for Robert returning home safely from the Battle of Agincourt in 1415. The tower of this church still stands today. The church was dedicated to the same saint as the well was – Saint Martin.

In 1757 there was a fire which completely gutted the nave of the church. The new nave which replaced it in 1759, was built in the shape of a hexagon. This gives an usual appearance to the church, with the hexagon and the square Medieval tower joining on to each other.

The church is a focal part of the well dressing celebrations when the wells are blessed at a service in the Nook outside the church gates.

The circular photograph is of a stained glass window in the church

The war memorial is in the shape of a cross

The font is a modern one. The original was removed when 'restorations' to the church were carried out in 1861, and then lost.

There are some attractive carvings on gravestones in the churchyard, including an hourglass, a sweet angel and one who 'waited patiently for the lord'

In a wooden frieze in the church is carved a pelican. The belief that the pelican pecked its breast to get blood and feed young, led to it being used as a symbol of Christ's sacrifice

Well Dressing: Pictures using nature.

The beautiful and delicate craft of well dressing is little known outside Derbyshire. This custom uses flowers, seeds, berries, leaves and other natural objects to create pictures which are then used to decorate wells, springs or even taps, between the months of May and September.

The custom possibly originated as a thanksgiving gesture to the gods and goddesses for the waters that are so necessary to life, or as an offering to ask these goddesses for favours, blessing or protection.

Pagans and Romans in Derbyshire would decorate the water sources with flowers or garlands. As Christianity spread in the area, the custom was absorbed by the church too and the wells were given saints to watch over them instead of goddesses.

Many well dressings today have a religious theme. The floral tributes are now in the form of pictures, not just garlands, and are very elaborate and skillfully done.

2004
STONEY
MIDDLETON

Make Space For Nature

BBC 2004

...take the young child and his mother, and flee into Egypt

An age old tradition of Derbyshire

Though the original origins are a little unclear, it is known that the custom died out for a while, perhaps under Puritan rule, and then was revived.

The revival began in the village of Tissington. Why it was in this village is unclear too, though theories are that the pure waters there preserved the villagers from the Black Death in the 14the century, or that the wells there kept flowing in a drought in 1615 when much of the other land was dry and crops were lost.

Some of the many villages that have the ever increasing celebrations of well dressings are Stoney Middleton, Tissington, Ashford-in-the-Water, Bakewell, Bradwell, Buxton, Youlgreave, Eyam, Hope and Wirksworth. It is often possible to go and see the well dressings being made.

The photographs show well dressings at Stoney Middleton, with close ups to show detail of petals etc.

How are the panels made?

■ A wooden board, often used year after year, is thrown into the local river to soak for a few days.

■ When removed, the board is filled with soft, wet clay. Because the board is wet, it stops the clay drying out too quickly. Salt is added to the clay to slow the drying process too. Nails are sometimes used to 'key' the clay together.

■ The outline of the picture is drawn in the clay. Different villages have various methods to do this, including wool, peppercorns, berries or pricking lines with a sharp instrument.

■ The picture is than coloured in using natural objects such as flower petals or sometimes whole flower heads, berries, leaves. twigs etc. pressed into the soft clay.

■ The finished picture will only last about a week before the clay dries out and cracks and the flowers fade.

The 'Plague Village'

The Parish Church of St. Lawrence at Eyam (pronounced 'eem')

A long told tale of sacrifice

In September 1665, Eyam was hit by a terrible affliction which killed many of the people there. The tale of this plague time has made the small and pretty village famous...

Plagues were often breaking out in England a few centuries ago, with the Great Plague of London in 1665 (and Great Fire of 1666 just after) perhaps the most famous. But the London plague is also said to have affected the quiet Peak District village of Eyam, hundreds of miles away.

A deadly parcel

Tradition has made the story of Eyam Plague almost mythical. The events in the sad and oft told tale unfold like this...

In the village of Eyam lived a widow named Mary Cooper. She lived with her two sons, near the church in what is now known as Plague Cottage.

Mary helped make ends meet by having a lodger there, whose name was George Viccars. George was an itinerant tailor and had cloth delivered to the cottage for him to make garments. One of the parcels of cloth he had delivered, in September 1665 was from London, where a plague was raging.

When the cloth arrived it was a little damp, so George spread it by the fire to dry out.

Though the people did not know at the time, it is widely told now that plague infected fleas from London's black rats *(Rattus rattus)* had been in the cloth and jumped off into the house and that it was these rat fleas that later bit the villagers and infected them too with the bubonic plague from London.

It was George who fell ill first from the strange illness and by September 7th he was dead and buried. Fifteen days later, Mary's son Edward died too, followed soon after by several of their neighbours. By October the death toll was rising and a few of the wealthier people fled the village. William Mompesson, the 28-year-old Rector of Eyam church, sent his children away to safety, but his wife Catherine, refused to go and stayed with her husband.

In June 1666, when people were still dying and it was clear the winter had not killed the plague germs, Mompesson and Thomas Stanley, a one-time non-conformist incumbent, called a public meeting. They urged the villagers not to run and, for the sake of containing the infection, to stay and isolate their village from the outside world. This is what happened, though perhaps the poorer people had no option anyway and if they tried to leave maybe other villages sent them back to Eyam for fear of infection.

Mompesson arranged for food and medical supplies to be left at arranged points around the village boundaries, from where they could be collected when the person who had delivered them was safely away. One place items were left was at a well on the village outskirts, now known as Mompesson's Well. Here money from the villagers to pay for the goods was left in running water to clean it. Another place was the Boundary Stone where coins were left in holes filled with vinegar, to try and disinfect them.

The Plague Cottages near the church at Eyam

Memorials to courage

Mompesson's Well

Tomb of Catherine Mompesson, who died on 25th August 1666

Church services in Eyam were halted, to lessen cross-contamination between people, and services were held in a nearby valley, Cucklett Delf. A service is still held there each year to commemorate the plague and the people who died.

So many people in Eyam village were dying that there were no people to bury the corpses and the clergy were too busy looking after the sick to do death services. Another proposal decided at the meeting in June was that families would bury their own dead near to home and as quickly as possible. One poignant example of this heartbreaking task is at the Riley Graves near Eyam, where a Mrs Hancock had the terrible task of digging graves for and burying her dead husband and six children in the space of eight days.

What the villagers went through can only be imagined by most of us, thankfully.

The plague had faded in Eyam by October 1666, but had taken with it the lives of 260 people, perhaps a third of the village. One of those who died was William Mompesson's wife, Catherine, though William survived and later moved to be rector at Eakring in Nottinghamshire.

A detail from the Mompesson tomb, a winged hourglass. Cave is Latin for beware

Memorial to the Rev. THOMAS STANLEY supporter of Rev. William Mompesson during the plague,

ALICE HANCOCK BVR AVG 9TH 1666

The Riley Graves of the Hancock family

So what was the plague at Eyam?

Much research in recent years has challenged the accepted tale of the plague at Eyam, as, for example, in an essay in the book Seven Blunders of the Peak edited by Professor Brian Robinson. He has researched and written widely on Eyam plague amongst many other subjects.

Plague was no stranger to Derbyshire before Eyam was hit, (but Eyam plague is most remembered because of the cutting off of the village) so the plague may have not even come from London, but from a nearer place and the cloth explanation is perhaps a coincidence. The first victim was, after all, a travelling tailor and could have already had the illness when he arrived at Eyam.

Much of the tale told today probably comes from a book written by a lifelong Eyam resident called William Wood, in 1842, called The History and Antiquities of Eyam. He writes of the plague, the bundle of cloth, etc in a melodramatic Victorian style that no doubt fuelled the version worthy of a novel we know today.

There has also been much discussion as to whether or not it was bubonic plague that killed the villagers, and that it could have been another illness. Cutting off the village would not have stopped the spread of bubonic plague, as rats and fleas do not take any notice of an isolation boundary. Ideas mooted as to other possible causes of death have ranged from severe measles, anthrax, or some form of viral haemorrhagic fever such as that caused by the Ebola virus.

A convincing argument against bubonic plague being brought from London to Eyam comes from studies by Prof.John Maunder of Cambridge University, which were communicated to Prof. Robinson: The bubonic plague is not passed on directly from flea to flea, but only into the flea itself from it sucking the blood of an infected black rat. The average lifespan of an infected flea is only 4 to 5 days – much shorter than the time for them to have arrived bundled up in cloth from London. Infected fleas would have been long dead by the time they got to Eyam. Any fleas hatched along the way would not have had any infected rat blood in them, nor could they have caught infection from the older fleas, so they would have been unable to infect the villagers with plague bacillus (Yersinia pestis) from London.

Whatever the truth, it is still the power of the accepted tale that wins over research, and the undoubted courage and plight of the villagers that wins over the hearts and sympathies of the many tourists.

Innocent sounding reminder...

Ring o' ring o' roses. A pocketful of posies
Atishoo, atishoo, we all fall down...

This well known children's nursery rhyme is thought to be about the plague and its symptoms:

'ring of roses' - the rash that a victim developed on their skin,
'pocket full of posies' - people carried nosegays or small bunches of herbs in an attempt to ward off the germs
'Atishoo' - sneezing was another symptom
'We all fall down' - the victim is overtaken by death

Eyam Museum

There is a museum in Eyam to tell the tale of the village, the people and the plague. The weathervane atop the building has a black rat on it – an appropriate reminder of the bearer of the village's sickness in the traditional tale of the plague.

The museum opened in 1994 and was extended and refurbished in 1997, with displays including those of Roman and Saxon life in the area, the plague and some supposed cures of the time, as well as a shop.

■ For more details about the museum, contact:
Eyam Museum, Hawkhill Road, Eyam, Derbyshire S32 5QP
Tel: (01433) 631371 or (01433) 630777 (school bookings)

On Church Street stands this elaborate barbeque for the annual sheep roast. In September, a whole sheep carcass is roasted in the open air on the old spit.

In the square is a reminder of bullbaiting. A bull was tied to a ring (still to be seen) and dogs harassed it. Bets were taken to see which dog pinned the bull down. Thankfully this practice was declared illegal in 1835

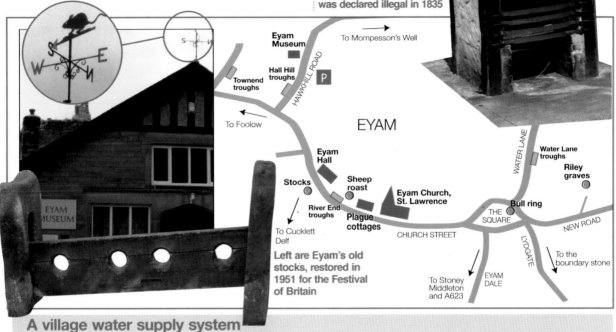

Left are Eyam's old stocks, restored in 1951 for the Festival of Britain

A village water supply system

There are several stone troughs to be seen throughout the village of Eyam. These are remains from one of the first examples of a water supply system in the country and were initiated by Colonel Francis Bradshaw of Bradshaw Hall in Eyam, in the year 1588. The system was used until the 1920s. The ruins of Bradshaw Hall still remain. The family fled the village during the plague. The hall was once used as a mill before becoming derelict.

The Parish Church of St. Lawrence

St Lawrence

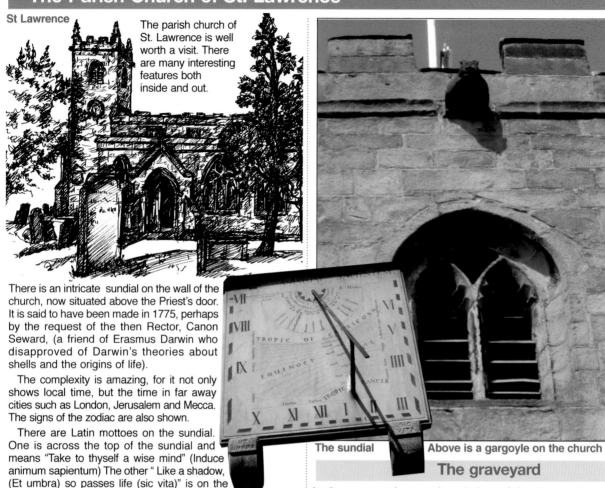

The parish church of St. Lawrence is well worth a visit. There are many interesting features both inside and out.

There is an intricate sundial on the wall of the church, now situated above the Priest's door. It is said to have been made in 1775, perhaps by the request of the then Rector, Canon Seward, (a friend of Erasmus Darwin who disapproved of Darwin's theories about shells and the origins of life).

The complexity is amazing, for it not only shows local time, but the time in far away cities such as London, Jerusalem and Mecca. The signs of the zodiac are also shown.

There are Latin mottoes on the sundial. One is across the top of the sundial and means "Take to thyself a wise mind" (Induce animum sapientum) The other " Like a shadow, (Et umbra) so passes life (sic vita)" is on the bottom corbel supports.

The sundial

Above is a gargoyle on the church

Wall paintings

On the walls of the nave are some paintings that are thought to date from around the 16th and 17th century, but may be on top of earlier artwork. Some of the paintings survived as they had been covered up during Puritan times, being rediscovered in the early 1960s. The remaining paintings were carefully conserved over a number of years.

The main subject of the paintings are of the ensigns of the twelve tribes of Israel, though there is a skeleton in the centre of the belfry arch that is thought to be earlier. He represents death, a reminder of our mortality.

The graveyard

In the graveyard are sad reminders of the plague victims, including the table tomb of William Mompesson's wife Catherine, who lost her life by refusing to leave her husband.

There is also the grave of cricketer Henry Bagshaw who played for Derbyshire and the MCC. He has a very appropriate epitaph written on the stone:

"Well played, for when the one Great Scorer comes to write against your name, he writes - not that you won or lost, but how you played the game"

Other gravestones include one for an artist and poet, which has a quill pen and a painter's palette, and some very old stones with cross and circle decoration.

The font (left) and some of the notable gravestones

Eyam Cross

Near the church, in the graveyard stands what is probably the Peak's best preserved high cross. It is thought to date from the 8th century.

The decoration has mainly knotwork and figures, plus scrollwork similar to that found on Bakewell cross, but there is also on archer figure to be found on this one.

The cross head has rounded spandrels and squared terminals and both faces have a circular panel, edged with roll moulding, in the centre.

The figures in the other panels on the cross head have wings, so are probably angels. They seem to be playing musical instruments. The angel figure in the central circle could be carrying a cross or staff.

One side of the cross has a figure that could be seen as the Virgin Mary. She has what looks like the holy child in her lap and one hand raised in blessing. The top of the figure's head is cut off a little showing some of the shaft is missing. The style of figures has pierced eyes and heavily folded drapery which is seen in the crosses of this area.

Half way down the shaft on one side, and under the figure described above, is a man with what looks like a horn in his arms. He has no wings so is not an angel, perhaps it is a figure associated with the lingering myths of the carvers, or some kind of priest equivalent. It could also perhaps be a well swaddled child he is carrying in his arms, not a horn.

A figure and knotwork detail from Eyam Cross

Eyam Hall

This fine old hall, opposite the village green, is still the family home of the Wright family, who have lived there for over 300 years. Thomas Wright built the house in 1671, for his son John.

Inside the house there are many fine paintings and tapestries and guided tours are available for the general public.

Also at the hall is a library with an 18th century love poem inscibed on a window pane, describing the charms of "Fanny ye pride of natures beauteous powers."

Other rooms include a bedroom, nursery, kitchen, wash house and Victorian dining room.

Next to the hall is the old stable block, now a Buttery and gift shop. There are also craft workshops to visit.

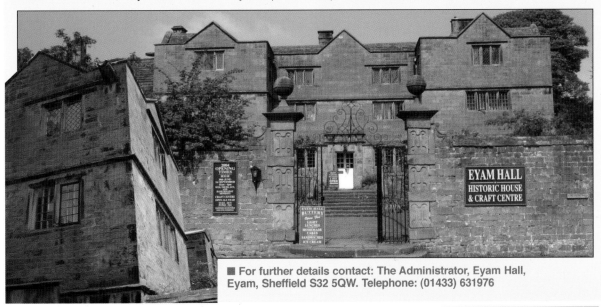

■ For further details contact: The Administrator, Eyam Hall, Eyam, Sheffield S32 5QW. Telephone: (01433) 631976

Padley Chapel

Padley Chapel. The ruins of the Manor House are to the right

Near the picturesque Padley Gorge, a popular walking spot, are the remains of an old hall, now partly restored as a chapel, which holds tales of religious secrecy and martyrdom...

Upper Padley, near Grindleford, is home to Padley Chapel, built within the gatehouse of a grand manor house which is now ruined

From hall to chapel

The Manor House which once stood at Upper Padley was built in the late 13th and early 14th century. When the sole heiress of the family owning the hall, Joan Padley, married Robert Eyre of Highlow towards the end of the 14th century, the Eyre family became the new owners.

Robert and Joan extended the hall, including the gatehouse which still stands.

In the 16th century the Manor of Padley was inherited by Anne Eyre. When she married Sir Thomas Fitzherbert, the Lord of Norbury the Fitzherbert family became the next owners. They continued to live at Norbury and gave Thomas' younger brother John the tenancy of the Manor House at Padley.

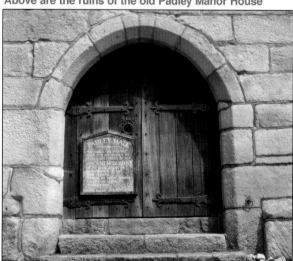

Above are the ruins of the old Padley Manor House

The model (left) shows how the Manor House probably looked and is on display inside the chapel. The circle marks where the chapel gable above is on the model

Thomas was a staunch Catholic and a recusant (one who refused to accept the new religion). He had been imprisoned for his beliefs. At this time, Queen Elizabeth I was on the throne and the religion of the country was that of the Protestant faith. It was illegal to be a Catholic priest, with any found practising tried for treason. Anyone found harbouring a priest was also committing an offence and tried for this crime.

The back of Padley Chapel (right) and the main door (left)

Dying for their faith

Thomas' brother John was also a recusant, but at Padley he thought he was more safe from prying eyes than his brother. He had a priest at Padley to say Mass, with any visits being in secret. On July 12 of 1588, however, the same year as war was imminent and rumours of a Spanish Armada were rife (and indeed came true), this came to an end.

The war fears made everyone wary of potential traitors and so anyone who was suspected of not following the Queen and her religion was in even more danger. The Earl of Shrewsbury led a party to raid Padley Manor to arrest John Fitzherbert, who was suspected of being a Catholic, and took him into custody.

When the party raided the hall, they found two Catholic priests there. The priests, Nicholas Garlick and Robert Ludlam, were found guilty of high treason and were hanged, drawn and quartered at St Mary's Bridge in Derby.

John Fitzherbert was found guilty of harbouring priests and jailed for life. He died whilst still in captivity, in 1590.

The Manor House fell into ruin. The gatehouse of the once fine home was used as a cowshed for a nearby farm, which meant that it was looked after and so survived better than the other parts of the building.

Later the gatehouse was converted into a chapel. A pilgrimage is made to this Padley Chapel every year, on the Sunday nearest 12th July, in memory of the priests who died so horribly for their faith and were later known as the Padley Martyrs. The chapel is also their shrine.

The chapel is usually open on Wednesdays and Sundays, 2pm to 4pm, April to September.

The foundations of the old Manor House can be seen around the back of the chapel.

Stones of the old Manor House (left) and the roof of the chapel (right)

Left, in the circle, is a window in the chapel showing the arrest of the two Catholic priests, Nicholas Garlick and Robert Ludlam

A stone in the ruins marks the spot where the old altar from the Manor House was found. It was placed in the chapel. Below are the remains of a spiral staircase

The back of Padley Chapel and the Manor House ruins. On the left is an outside altar for services to remember the Padley Martyrs.

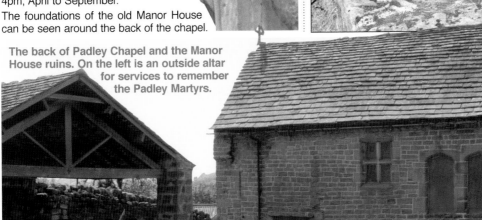

Around Padley Gorge

THE NATIONAL TRUST

LONGSHAW ESTATE
PADLEY GORGE

PLEASE
KEEP TO THE PATHS
DO NOT CLIMB THE WALLS
KEEP DOGS ON LEADS
OBSERVE THE BYELAWS ON
THE BACK OF THIS NOTICE

You may spot a Pied Flycatcher as you walk around Padley. These birds live in woodland habitats

Ruins of Padley Hall

Padley Chapel

Padley Mill

Houses

Padley Gorge

Totley Tunnel

Grindleford Cafe

To Grindleford

Station approach

Grindleford Station

Trains from Sheffield stop at the station at Grindleford

The countryside around Padley Gorge is beautiful, with dappled sunlight, bubbling waters and strewn boulders. The station for the village of Grindleford is nearby. This village takes its name from the grindstone industry and the fact that it has long been an ancient crossing point, or ford, on the River Derwent.

Near the station is a favourite haunt of hungry or weary walkers – Grindleford Station Cafe. The cafe is housed in the old Victorian station building of 1898. The old wooden ticket barrier is still in place. This is a great and characterful stop for chip butties or some other fortifying treat as you wander the area or stop to watch trains re-appear from the Totley Tunnel entrance next to it. The tunnel was built between 1888 and 1893.

Walking up from the cafe towards Padley Chapel, the path passes the pretty Padley Mill, now a private residence.

The Totley Tunnel, above left. Right is Grindleford Station Cafe, great for a hearty meal stop or mug of steaming coffee

Stone cutters

The Peak District is scattered with the legacy of the stone cutters, from millstones to dam stones. Unfinished or complete millstones can be seen on many a walk, abandoned to nature...

Just along from Padley Chapel, the path continues into an area once a hive of industry. Here is a veritable millstone grave-yard, as well as remains of a quarry railway.

The millstone heritage

As you enter the Peak District National Park, a millstone is the symbol chosen to welcome visitors. This is a very appropriate choice as it serves to commemorate one of the major industries carried out in the area using the local stone.

The appearance of many of the edges in Derbyshire has been created by the chunks of rock taken from them to produce millstones. Indeed the name of Millstone Edge, overlooking Hathersage, is a bit of a giveaway!

The rocks of the area have long been used by man for the task of grinding, from old hand querns, to corn mills and later for the grinding wheels used in cutlery making (shown right). Some were

One use of the stones was for for cutlery grinding

also used for crushing lead ore, like the one at Odin Mine at Castleton. Early settlers in the Iron Age used the querns or hand turned stones to grind corn (above). It could be that the wood name 'Yarncliffe' near Grindleford is a corruption of the name 'querncliff' a cliff from which the querns were made. Later the querns gave way to millstones, with larger ones turned by animals such as a donkey. The animal would be attached to the stone by a wooden shaft and rope and would walk in a circle. Stones in mills would be turned by water power. The mills used pairs of stones to grind the grain between.

Abandoned stone in the Peak District cut by hands long passed

Scattered stones

The Peak District was one of the largest producers of the millstones that were sent to many other places, including the continent, usually via the old port of Bawtry.

The Peak District was so popular for millstones because of a useful property of the local rock, which became known as Millstone Grit. When this rock is freshly cut from the ground, it is relatively soft and can therefore be shaped better. However, when it dries out and stands exposed to air, it hardens and therefore develops hard wearing properties.

Daniel Defoe in his book A Tour Through England and Wales, writes: *"Millstones and grindstones, in very great quantities, are brought down and shipped off here and so carry'd by sea to Hull and to London and even to Holland also. This makes Bautry (Bawtry) Wharf be famous"*

The seventeenth century was probably the peak of the industry and it carried on until around the early 1900s.

These stones are to be seen at Stanage Edge

Stones now poking out from grass or bracken look like a giant's buttons. Some are cracked and would have been abandoned by the makers as useless Some are neatly left as if the maker had gone for lunch and forgotten to come back. Possibly they were piled here for loading onto carts or sledges. Another way of moving stones was by putting a small tree trunk or wood pole through the hole in the middle of two stones and pushing them along like wheels on an axle.

Walking down from the Surprise View on the A625, through a little stile on the left as the road leads towards Hathersage from Sheffield, is the easiest way to find what looks like a millstone graveyard at Bolehill. It is like an industrial version of the Marie Celeste with dozens of stones just left there by hewers. Once over the stile it is an easy, level, grassy path.

These stones are at Bolehill, near the Surprise View

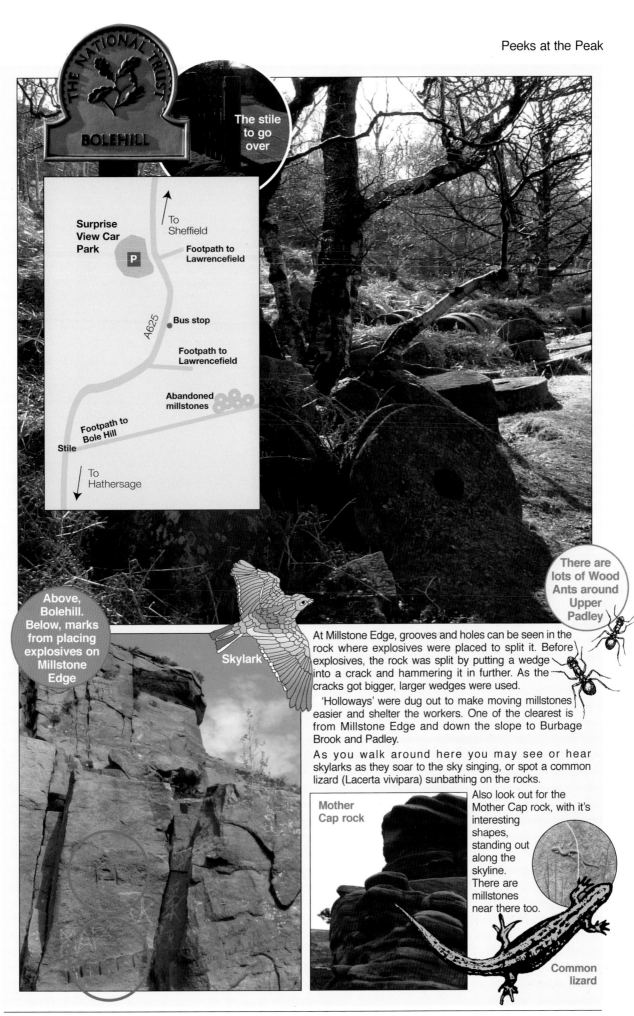

BOLEHILL

The stile to go over

Surprise View Car Park

P

To Sheffield

Footpath to Lawrencefield

A625

Bus stop

Footpath to Lawrencefield

Abandoned millstones

Footpath to Bole Hill

Stile

To Hathersage

There are lots of Wood Ants around Upper Padley

Above, Bolehill. Below, marks from placing explosives on Millstone Edge

Skylark

At Millstone Edge, grooves and holes can be seen in the rock where explosives were placed to split it. Before explosives, the rock was split by putting a wedge into a crack and hammering it in further. As the cracks got bigger, larger wedges were used.

'Holloways' were dug out to make moving millstones easier and shelter the workers. One of the clearest is from Millstone Edge and down the slope to Burbage Brook and Padley.

As you walk around here you may see or hear skylarks as they soar to the sky singing, or spot a common lizard (Lacerta vivipara) sunbathing on the rocks.

Mother Cap rock

Also look out for the Mother Cap rock, with it's interesting shapes, standing out along the skyline. There are millstones near there too.

Common lizard

From millstones to dam stones

Just a little after Padley Chapel, walking from the Grindleford direction, is a sunken and overgrown dip. This once carried the twin tracks of an incline railway. The now quiet spot would once have been noisy from wagons trundling up and down.

The wagons were full of stone from the Bolehill quarry just above, when the stone once used for millstones was being cut to make stones for the great engineering project of the dams at Howden and Derwent.

When the stone was put into the wagons, these wagons then needed to be taken down to join the main railway line below and on to the dam site, via The Bamford & Howden Railway on the last stage of their journey. They were lowered by means of the inclined 1 in 3 railway. The weight of a heavily filled wagon going down would pull up an empty one from the bottom.

The old incline railway site is now an overgrown dip and often overlooked

PHOTO: Reproduced by kind permission of Prof. Brian Robinson. (Copyright: Prof. Brian Robinson)

In this photograph of the railway incline, a wagon full of stone is descending and at the same time is hauling the distant empty wagon up the hill, via cables passing over the winding drum that is just over the top of the incline

Remains of the wheel house

If you walk up alongside the steep but direct path by the incline you come to the top, where there are remains of a large stone structure. (The path from the Surprise View also leads to here eventually). This is the old winding drum house, where the self acting wheel or drum holding the heavy steel cables attached to the wagons was housed. The huge drum would have been between the walls that still stand there today, as seen in the photograph, right.

PHOTO: Reproduced by kind permission of Prof. Brian Robinson. (Copyright: Prof. Brian Robinson)

Left is what is left of the structure today, right is how it looked when the railway was in full swing

The standard gauge railway here was a hive of activity. As well as the railway, there were workshops, water storage tanks and also bungalows, a recreation room and messroom for the workmen. The railway also had steam powered travelling cranes, which were used to move the cut stone blocks from the quarry face and into the trucks.

Small steam locomotives were also used. The one in the photograph of the drum house above is either 'Bobs' or 'MacDonald'.

At the bottom of the incline, the trucks were shunted into sidings and then hauled by locomotives of the Midland Railway on their main line, to Thornhill, near Bamford. Here special sidings had been constructed, known as 'Waterworks Sidings'.

From here the trucks were taken to the dam sites by locomotives from the Derwent Valley Water Board, who were building the dams, over their own line, the Bamford & Howden Railway.

Carrying on up the grassy path to the left of the winding drum house and cutting up to the right over zig-zagging old railway track beds, now grassed over, leads to the quarry face.

'Bole' is a common word in names around the Peak District and Sheffield and is derived from an earlier use of the area, lead mining. Boles were depressions in the ground where the lead ore was smelted.

These boles were put on hilltops as the winds were stronger up there and so it was better for fanning and getting the fires up to heat with a good draw.

Dambuilders

A tower of Derwent Dam pictured from Fairholmes

The stones cut from Bolehill Quarry, near Grindleford, were used to build the mighty dams of the Upper Derwent Valley, great feats of engineering and skill...

Standing by Howden Dam today, the wall and towers soar above as if they have been there forever, and it is hard to imagine the landscape without them.

Construction begins

As cities and industries expanded in the 19th century, the water needed by the population and factories grew and it was to serve this increasing need that dams to impound the necessary reservoirs were constructed.

The Upper Valley of the Derwent was considered ideal to use for reservoirs to supply the surrounding areas due to it being deep and surrounded by gritstone edges. In 1899, the Derwent Valley Water Board (DVWB) was set up with the purpose of impounding reservoirs in the valley to supply Derby, Leicester Nottingham and Sheffield with potable water.

Two reservoirs, Howden and Derwent, with their accompanying huge dams, were impounded between 1901 and 1916.

In November 1901 the first steps were taken when the DVWB bought the land at Bole Hill to quarry and cut stone and set up the work site with its standard gauge railway and incline. (Before they could do this, they had to clear away debris left by the millstone cutters of earlier years).

The best stone was cut to be used for the outsides of the dams that were on show, The inferior stones were kept for the interior and small ones for crushing up to make concrete. The first wagon loaded with millstone grit stone destined for the Derwent Valley was sent down the incline railway on 23rd May, 1903. About 430 men were employed at this prolific site.

The train below, Nogi, was a locomotive used at Bole Hill Quarry. Delivered in 1905, it was moved to Howden in 1910 when the quarry closed and then to the Derwent site in 1913. In this picture, the engine's side facing the camera has been greased and decorated by hand with a scale-like pattern

PHOTO: Courtesy of/ copyright Prof. Brian Robinson

Viaduct built at Ashopton to carry the Bamford & Howden Railway. This area is now hidden under the Ladybower Reservoir

The stone was then taken to Waterworks Sidings, as mentioned in the previous chapter. From here the specially built Bamford & Howden Railway (standard gauge) took it to the dam site. Three viaducts – at Ashopton, Fairholmes and Birchinlee – were also constructed using timber trestles on stone piers, to carry sections of this railway.

Work on the first dam at Howden began in July 1901, with pumps clearing water from the excavations as they got lower and lower. Work at the Derwent site began in July 1902.

PHOTO: This and the one of Nogi courtesy of/ copyright Prof. Brian Robinson

The Howden Dam as constructed by July 1908

A mighty feat

PHOTO: Courtesy of/ copyright Prof. Brian Robinson

A mobile support tower for the cableway or 'Blondin' across the Derwent site. Lifting gear is seen suspended from the cables

PHOTO: Courtesy of/copyright Prof. Brian Robinson

Laying the last of the cast-iron pipes in October 1909 to complete the section of the water delivery aqueduct between the Derwent Dam and Grindleford

To help extract rubble from the excavation sites and then later get the stone into the dam sites, special cableways were constructed. These were called 'Blondins' after the trapeze artist and tightrope walker. The cables were made of steel wires and had a circumference of 7 inches, with a carrying capacity of six tons. These cables were suspended over the valley from timber towers on the hillsides. The cableways were driven by steam engines.

By December 1910, the quarry at Bole Hill had been shut down and the site was dismantled. It finally closed in September 1914. In its short life the quarry had sent about a million tons of stone out for the dams. (The DVWB gave the site to the National Trust in 1947).

Water flows

On New Year's Day 1912, control valves in the east tower of the Howden Dam were closed and the reservoir began to form. The formal opening of the dam, when the water was released for public use, was on for 5 September 1912. King George was unable to attend, so the ceremony was carried out by the then chairman of the DVWB, Sir Edward H Fraser. There were hundreds of people present who had arrived on specially provided trains, hymns were sung as a band played and there was a grand tea in a marquee afterwards for guests, workers and their families.

Four years later, the Derwent Dam was brought into commission, without any ceremony, perhaps because of the subdued atmosphere of the First World War, going on at the time.

Now these hard won feats of engineering and vision are popular with visitors who come to see the man made beauty of the reservoirs, as well as the natural beauty of the countryside.

The area is well used for recreation such as cycle riding. There is a Visitor Centre at Fairholmes where bikes can be hired, refreshments and books etc bought. This Visitor Centre and the adjacent car parks are built on the site of the rubble excavated when the Derwent Dam was built.

■ Fairholmes Visitor Centre/cycle hire, Derwent, Bamford, Sheffield S33 0AQ Tel: (01433) 650953/651261

■ email: cyclehire@peakdistrict.gov.uk

A canine memorial

Near Derwent Reservoir is a stone in memory of a faithful dog. The sheepdog Tip stood guard over her master's dead body in the deep snow on Howden Moor for 15 weeks, from 12th December 1953 to 27th March 1954. She never recovered fully from her sad sentry duty and died just a year later.

The stone was put there by public subscription in memory of Tip and her master.

The photo of the little dog, superimposed here on a photo of the memorial, was in the archives of Sheffield Newspapers, and captioned 'Tip', but, if it is the very same Tip that waited on the moors, I am not sure

PHOTOS: Courtesy of Sheffield Newspapers

The Dambusters

The Derwent Dams are known by many today for the much publicised connection with the heroic RAF 617 Squadron, 'The Dambusters', though the scale of the role has sometimes been exaggerated.

Practising low level flying techniques to prepare for dropping Barnes Wallis' famous 'bouncing bomb' depth charge to destroy German dams during World War 2 was a necessity for

PHOTO: Courtesy of Sheffield Newspapers

Lancaster Bomber flyover at Derwent in 1977

the 617 Squadron, who were due to carry out the daring mission.

Just days before the planned raid, some of the bomber pilots were sent to Derwent Dam in 1943 for this practice, but other pilots went to other stretches of water and Derwent was certainly not the only place used.

Before this final practice, Guy Gibson, the Squadron Leader, and two of his senior officers had carried out two flights in Lancaster Bombers to look over the Derwent area and try out the flight for themselves.

The Derwent Dam was similar in construction to one of the German dams and so was used to practice aiming techniques, with the two towers being used to test the triangular wooden bomb sight that was being developed for the raid, in order to be able to position the drop of the bouncing depth charge correctly.

The raid on the German dams was carried out during the night of 16-17 May 1943. For many of those men who flew in the Lancaster Bombers to carry out that raid, it was their final act.

The Derwent Dam's connection with the brave pilots has been celebrated over the years with the flyover of an awesome Lancaster Bomber, a wonderful and stirring sight.

Even though the Derwent Valley played just a small part in the story of the Dambusters, it forms a fitting and impressive focus to remind us of the raid and also of the many who lost their lives in the war.

There is a museum in the West Tower of the Derwent Dam which has memorabilia related to the 617 Squadron.

■ Dam Busters Museum, West Tower, Derwent Valley Dam.
■ Open: usually 10am-4pm, Sundays and Bank Holidays

Ladybower

The building of the last dam in this grand scheme by the DVWB, at Ladybower, commenced in 1935 and continued through World War 2.

Ladybower looks very different from the other dams in the Derwent Valley, less gothic and more modern. It does not have an overflow that gives an awesome cascade down the dam, as at Howden and Derwent, but has two funnel shaped overflows, one at each side of the dam that look like giant plug holes.

This final reservoir at Ladybower caused great controversy because the impounding of it swallowed up the villages of Derwent and Ashopton (pictured below).

The human remains in Derwent churchyard were exhumed and reburied at Bamford. The tower of the church had been left intact and once made an eerie sight poking out of the waters like a finger marking a Peak District Atlantis when the waters were very low. It was finally totally demolished in 1947.

The 17th century Derwent Hall, was also a victim. It had become a Youth Hostel in 1931 and is now but a memory under the water.

The ancient packhorse bridge at Derwent was moved stone by stone and rebuilt at Slippery Stones (above), at the head of Howden Reservoir.

The dam was completed in 1943 but it took two years to fill the reservoir. The official opening was on 25 September 1945, when King George VI and the then Queen (our present Queen's late mother) did the honours.

The King and Queen with Alderman Sir Albert Atkey, then the Chairman of the DVWB, at the opening of the Ladybower Reservoir on September 25, 1945

PHOTO: Courtesy of Sheffield Newspapers

PHOTO: Courtesy of Sheffield Newspapers

This stone shepherd (left) with his clay pipe is called Peeping Tom. He once peeped from the parapet of Derwent Hall's stables. Today he is found in the Youth Hostel at Castleton looking out from behind the reception desk

Tin Town

The building of the dams was such a huge project that the workers, destined to be there a long time, had a village specially built for them. The workers were known as 'navvies' which is short for 'navigators' a name coined when these nomadic, hard working and often exploited construction workers built the navigations (canals).

The village that became home to about 1000 of these navvies and their families was called Birchinlee, and was midway between the two dam sites. The village took its name from Birchinlee Farm which stood on the site.

Birchinlee was a fully fledged community, with nearly 100 buildings including shops, a hospital, pub, meeting house, police station and school, as well as the accommodation huts. These huts and other buildings had corrugated iron walls and roofs – earning the village the nickname of 'Tin Town'. The accommodation, however, was very well appointed inside, with wood lined walls, paraffin lighting and furnishings as good as any middle-class Victorian house – indeed the word 'huts' doesn't do them justice!.

There is little to see at the site of this once busting village today. When the reservoir work had been finished, the buildings were no longer needed. Demolition of the huts began in December 1913 and by August 1914 half of them had gone.

PHOTO: Courtesy of/ copyright Prof. Brian Robinson

Some huts were sold to the War Office, some were sold locally. One can still be seen in the village of Hope, where it is now used as a hairdresser's salon on Edale Road.

The Birchinlee Farm house was demolished in 1914 and stones from it were used as pitching on the wall at the foot of the Howden Dam, to protect the Howden to Derwent aqueduct.

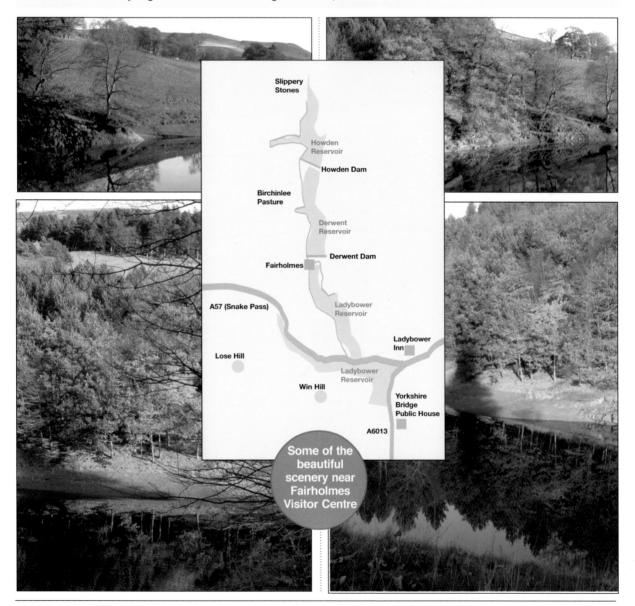

Slippery Stones

Howden Reservoir

Howden Dam

Birchinlee Pasture

Derwent Reservoir

Derwent Dam

Fairholmes

A57 (Snake Pass)

Ladybower Reservoir

Lose Hill

Ladybower Inn

Ladybower Reservoir

Win Hill

Yorkshire Bridge Public House

A6013

Some of the beautiful scenery near Fairholmes Visitor Centre

Arbor Low

A spectacular 4000 year old prehistoric monument lies in the fields of Derbyshire, spread upon the grass like a huge, silent clockface...

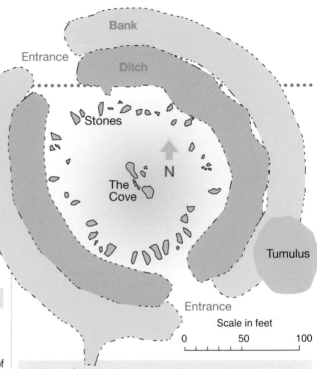

Set in a field behind a farm, near Monya... is an ancient stone circle, or henge. It i... known as the Stonehenge of the North ... and consists of a bank 250ft in diameter, abou... 7ft high, with a 30ft wide, 5ft deep quarry ditch.

The Mighty Henge

This enigmatic monument, 1,200ft above sea level, is one of the county's chief prehistoric monuments. Recumbent lime-stones lie surrounded by a ditch in a wild and open place.

The ditch is broken by two entrances, and encloses a circle of around 40 stones, none of which is standing. The largest stone is about 13ft long. The name Arbor Low is thought to derive from the anglo Saxon **Eorthburh Hlaw,** which merely means earthwork hill. This ancient structure would have amazed people through the centuries. When the Romans came, the site was already 2,500 years old.

It is not known whether the stones were originally upright. In 1758 it is recorded that one man remembered the stones standing, but when the circle was excavated no evidence of holes that the stones would have rested in was found. It could be that no deep pits were dug to stand them in so no traces are left. If they were just set in shallow foundations, this could explain why they have all fallen, with many of the stones break-ing on impact with the ground. There are some stumps of stone which could support this theory, being the lower broken part of the recumbent stones. It is an exposed site so loosely set stones could have blown over. At the centre is a U shaped clus-ter of stones, called the cove. This has two of the biggest stones. Near these stones a male skeleton was found.

No one knows why these henges, the most famous of which is Stonehenge, were built. Perhaps they were the enclosures for rituals or communal gatherings. Some people think they were used for astronomical calculations.

Around Arbor Low

Close to the area of the monument are burial mounds, or barrows. One such barrow is built into the bank near the Southern entrance of the ditch. This was excavated by local historian Thomas Bateman, in 1845. In it he found cremations, a bone pin and two food vessels within a cist (small enclosure of stones).

A shoulder-blade and an antler of a large red deer were found and, in a cist in the centre were discovered human bones, a kidney-shaped piece of flint, a pin made from the leg bone of a small deer and a spherical piece of iron pyrites. At the west end of the cist were two clay urns, shaped and decorated in very different ways plus a frag-ment of a third.

In 1901-2 Arbor Low was excavated again, this time by a man called H. St George Gray. He dug the bank and ditch and found flint tools, ox bones, two arrowheads and traces of fires.

Scale in feet
0   50   100

Gib Hill

A low bank and ditch, that may have been built at a later date, run towards Arbor Low from the south. Also, 350 yards to the south lies a mount known as Gib Hill. This is a large barrow, about 10ft high. This is how Bateman describes it:

"Its height, immense size and remote antiquity are calculated to impress the reflecting mind with feelings of wonder and admiration."

The name may come from the fact that a gibbet was once placed on the mound, but nobody knows for sure. It seems to have been built in two phases. An earlier neolithic (4000 - 2000 BC) oval barrow was enlarged by building a mound over the top of it. This mound was probably built in the early Bronze age, (2000 - 700 BC)..

In this mound, Bateman found a stone cist containing a cremation and a food vessel, as well as an arrow-head of flint, two and a half inches long. The cist had probably been placed on top of the earlier barrow, before the bigger mound was put on top. When the exca-vation was taking place, the cist, with its heavy stones, crashed down and crushed a food vessel and the remains of the human crema-tion which had been inside it. Bateman put this central stone cist in his home grounds in a village nearby, but it has now been re-erected and the capstone is just visible at the crest of the barrow.

To the north west of Gib Hill there are traces of a 180ft diameter ditched enclo-sure and bank that may be another henge monument. The site is managed by English Heritage: Northampton Office NN1 1UH

There is a request for a small donation, which can be left in a tin by the farm. There is a small car park.

Getting There

Take the Monyash road from Bakewell (B5055). Turn left towards Youlgreave. The site is signposted off this road and is at the back of the farm over a stile.

"the solitude of the place and the boundless view of an uncultivated country are such as almost carry the observer back through a multitude of centuries..."
Thomas Bateman

Thomas Bateman

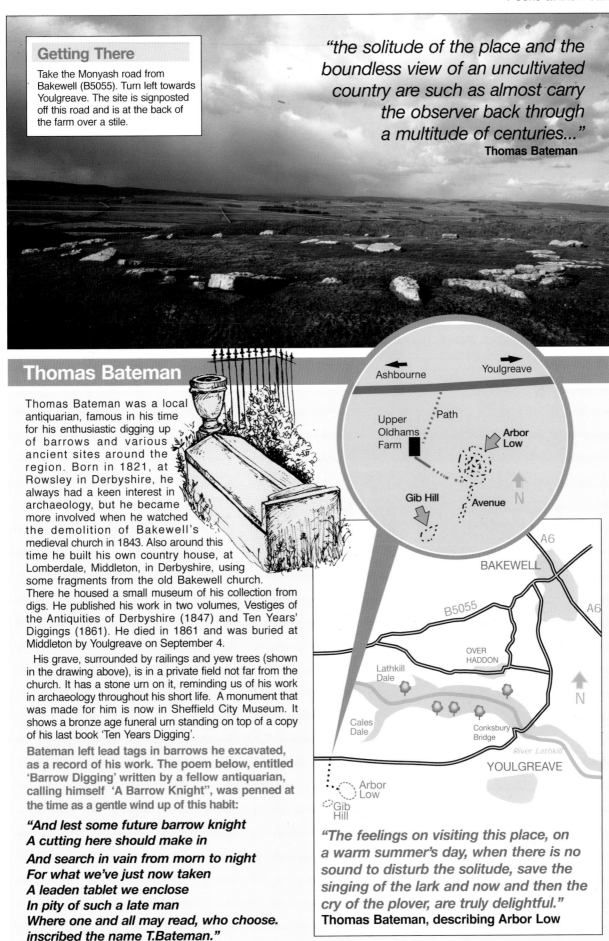

Thomas Bateman was a local antiquarian, famous in his time for his enthusiastic digging up of barrows and various ancient sites around the region. Born in 1821, at Rowsley in Derbyshire, he always had a keen interest in archaeology, but he became more involved when he watched the demolition of Bakewell's medieval church in 1843. Also around this time he built his own country house, at Lomberdale, Middleton, in Derbyshire, using some fragments from the old Bakewell church. There he housed a small museum of his collection from digs. He published his work in two volumes, Vestiges of the Antiquities of Derbyshire (1847) and Ten Years' Diggings (1861). He died in 1861 and was buried at Middleton by Youlgreave on September 4.

His grave, surrounded by railings and yew trees (shown in the drawing above), is in a private field not far from the church. It has a stone urn on it, reminding us of his work in archaeology throughout his short life. A monument that was made for him is now in Sheffield City Museum. It shows a bronze age funeral urn standing on top of a copy of his last book 'Ten Years Digging'.

Bateman left lead tags in barrows he excavated, as a record of his work. The poem below, entitled 'Barrow Digging' written by a fellow antiquarian, calling himself 'A Barrow Knight", was penned at the time as a gentle wind up of this habit:

"And lest some future barrow knight
A cutting here should make in

And search in vain from morn to night
For what we've just now taken
A leaden tablet we enclose
In pity of such a late man
Where one and all may read, who choose.
inscribed the name T.Bateman."

"The feelings on visiting this place, on a warm summer's day, when there is no sound to disturb the solitude, save the singing of the lark and now and then the cry of the plover, are truly delightful."
Thomas Bateman, describing Arbor Low

Another sacred landscape

Nine Stone Close, the Hermit's Cave and Robin Hood's Stride

On Harthill Moor, off the road from Bakewell to Winster (B5056), and not far from The Druid Inn, is found the stone circle called Nine Stone Close. Contrary to the name, there are now only four large stones left, one being eight feet high and nine feet in circumference. They are sometimes known as the Grey Ladies, said in folklore to dance by the light of a full moon. One stone is in use nearby as a gatepost.

Overlooking the stones is a natural rock outcrop called Robin Hood's Stride. Another name for it is Mock Beggars Hall, as the shape resembles a hall with tall chimneys. These 'chimneys' are called Weasel and Inaccesible by climbers.

Also nearby stands a rock formation called Cratcliffe Tor. A path here winds to an old hermit's cave with a crucifix carved upon the right hand wall. The carving is unusual as it has foliage carved around the cross.

The cave is hidden behind the boughs of an ancient yew. In the cave is a small niche, probably to hold a lamp.

The old shelter is thought to be from the fourteenth century, perhaps used as a stop off on the ancient trackway called the Portway, which passes between the tor and Robin Hood's Stride. Below is a picture of the cave entrance.

Nine Stone Close, with Robin Hood's Stride in the background

The Crucifix at the hermit's cave

The hermit's cave entrance

Robin Hood's Stride

Some other nearby Circles

Other stone circles in the area are those on Barbrook Moor, off to the right through white gates on the A621 Owler Bar to Baslow road. The first encountered to the right of the footpath from the road is Barbrook I. It is an isolated spot, very atmospheric and hardly any signs of man can be seen from here, even though the road is so close. The circle consists of a ring of low-standing stones, with a damaged low bank around them.

A little further along from Barbrook I is Barbrook II. It consists of a rubble bank, with a ring of standing stones set along the inside of it. These are smaller than at Barbrook I, except for one which is 3ft high. The bank has an original entrance about 10ft wide to the north east. In the centre of the circle is a small cairn and a cist, both from around 1800BC, (mid Bronze Age). There are other circles on the moor but they are harder to find. Although there is a path, the circles are in a wildlife sanctuary, so please respect this. The area is managed by Peak District National Park Authority.

On Froggatt Edge, on the left near a gate leading up to the edge from the road, can be found another stone circle. It is quiite overgrown. One stone is much taller than the others.

Nine Stone Close and one of the stones close up

Small stone circle on Froggatt Edge

Around Stanton Moor

Nine Ladies and Stanton Moor

The other famous stone circle in the Peak area is that of the Nine Ladies. It stands in a sheltered hollow near the northern end of Stanton Moor, near Stanton in Peak, off the A6. The circle in fact consists of ten stones, about 2 to 3 feet in height. 30ft in diameter. Its purpose is unknown. The name Nine Ladies was given before a tenth stone in the bank was uncovered due to erosion in the last 15 years. About 130ft from the circle is the 3ft high 'King Stone' set on its own. A local legend tells that the stones are ladies turned to rock for dancing on the sabbath and the King Stone was once their fiddler.

Around sixty burial mounds have been found on the moor, often with cremation urns and flint tools. They were excavated many years ago by local archaeologist J C Heathcote and his son J P Heathcote.

A photograph of Nine Ladies circle on Stanton Moor

Carvings. On some of the rocks on Stanton Moor are carvings, including a deeply cut letter Y and a coronet with the date 1826. This is to commemorate the Duke of York. These carvings were put there by the Thornhill Family of nearby Stanton Hall.

Earl Grey Tower.

Also to be found on the moor is a 30ft high. square brick tower (left). This was built in tribute to Earl Grey, who carried the reform bill through parliament. Over the door is inscribed his name and the date 1832. Nearby are the Duke of York stone, with the coronet and the inscription Y 1826 and one inscribed G 1834.

Right: an urn found in one of the burial mounds on Stanton Moor

The Cork Stone

On the western side of the moor is a large stone (right) with holes that have been added to aid climbing up to the top of it. This is known as the Cork Stone.

Rowter Rocks

Near to Stanton Moor, at the bottom end of the village of Birchover, and behind the Druid Inn, are some amazing rocks. These gritstone features have natural rock basins, though the hand of man has added quirky 'improvements'. Some large stones, as you climb the path at the back of the Druid Inn, have socket marks on. These may indicate that wooden structures were built here, with these holes made for putting the poles in. As you wander around these fascinating rocks there can be seen carved out chambers. Some tales say this was a prison for those awaiting druidical sacrifice. There is no evidence of this however.

The Rev. Thomas Eyre, who lived close by in the 17th century, converted these rocks into a retreat. He carved rooms, arm chairs and steps to link the different areas together.

Opposite these rocks and the Druid Inn is the small, usually locked, Rowter Chapel. The outside has lovely carvings.

Dragon and foliage carved on the church at Birchover

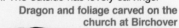

Some of the carved stairs at Rowter Rocks, in Birchover

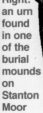

A nearby salamander

The village of Youlgreave, (or Youlgrave), lies a little way from Birchover and was once a centre for lead mining, then gritstone quarrying. The village has many fine buildings. There is also a circular construction called the fountain, built in 1829, which once held water for the village and an 1887 Co-Op building now a Youth Hostel opposite it .

One of the oldest and prettiest buildings is a hall built around 1640, but the dominating feature of this pretty place is the church, All Saint's. It is partly Norman, with a 15th century tower. The font is late Norman period. It is unusual as it has an extra holder on the side, for putting in oil. This is called a stoup. A wonderful salamander, carved upaide down, decorates the stone, his head near the stoup.

Another feature of the church is a miniature alabaster effigy to Thomas Cokayne. Under his head is a helmet with a cock's head, a pun on the family name. The effigy is thought to be small because he died young in a brawl in 1488, before his father.

An effigy of a knight, from around the 13th century, and thought to be Sir John Rossington, is also impressive and the oldest monument in the church. He lies cross legged, with a heart in his hands and his feet resting on a dog.

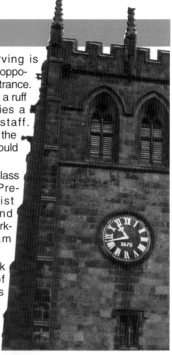

Carving on the wall that could be a pilgrim

A small figure carving is found on the wall opposite the main entrance. The figure wears a ruff collar and carries a pouch and a staff. It has been dated to the 12th century and could represent a pilgrim.

The east window glass is designed by Pre-Raphaelite artist Burne Jones and made in the craft workshops of William Morris.

Other features to look out for are carved roof bosses, a carved reredos (a back of altar decoration) and a piscina (holy water holder) which is decorated with a carved head.

Some features in the church of All Saint's at Youlgreave:
A. The font with stoup and salamander B. The effigy of Thomas Cockayne
C. The Pre Raphaelite windows D. Effigy of a knight
E. A lion carving on one of the seats

Carl Wark

The enigmatic feature known as Carl Wark is a Peak District landmark, but there is debate as to the purpose of the walls and boulders placed there long ago...

Coming from Sheffield along or near the A625, the breathtaking hills of the Peak District open out before you, with Carl Wark to the right.

Fortress or not?

Carl Wark is one of the outstanding landmarks in the splendid view of the Peak District and Derbyshire as you leave Sheffield and head out into the countryside. It stands just off A625 Sheffield to Hathersage Road, near the Fox House Inn.

It is often written that Carl Wark is an old hill fort, but this is a much debated subject. It may have been altered and added to at various times and there is no wood so far found to be able to date things accurately.

It may have been built or perhaps just re-enforced as a response to invasion when the Romans came, to try and protect the local people. Now it is a scheduled ancient monument.

Carl Wark sits on a natural rock outcrop. Next to it is Higger Tor. Though Higger Tor is more imposing, Carl Wark seems to have been reinforced and used because its natural contours made it easier to build on and protect.

There are large boulders placed and a dry stone rampart to the west at the weakest point. There seems to have been a narrow artificial entrance which could be more easily defended. The natural stone rockfaces themselves would have offered a lot of protection.

If it was used as a fort it could perhaps have had wooden walls or palisades like other iron age forts but no evidence is known to have been found so far.

Toad's Mouth

This rock formation is just at the bend of the road at the bridge as you pass Fox House on the way to Hathersage on the A625. It does look like a large toad sitting hunched up and watching the passing traffic and hikers..

Longshaw

Around the Fox House Inn is land now looked after by the National Trust, the Longshaw Estate. Longshaw Lodge was once the Duke of Rutland's shooting estate but was bought by public subscription in 1927 and presented to the Trust. It is a large estate, stretching to Grindleford and including Millstone Edge and Bole Hill. The lodge now holds a visitor centre and tea shop, a good place to rest and eat as you look over the countryside to Carl Wark. There is a pleasant walk around the lodge and a large pond there. The estate is well known for the Longshaw Sheepdog Trials, held every September.

■ Longshaw Visitor Centre: 01433 631708
■ Email: longshaw@nationaltrust.org.uk

The Fox House Inn, sited nerar Carl Wark and Longshaw

Sir Joseph Paxton

The much admired Chatsworth

Paxton is one of those people that seemed to have had an almost superhuman amount of energy. Once a gardener at Chatsworth he went on to build the world famous Crystal Palace...

Chatsworth is probably one of the grandest and best known stately homes in the country. Joseph Paxton is one of the people who helped create the gardens there.

A Stately Mansion

The House and gardens at Chatsworth have long been a popular place to visit and admire. The poet Wordsworth wrote :

"Chatsworth! thy stately mansion and the pride Of thy domain, strange contrast do present To house and home in many a craggy rent Of the wild Peak..."

But this chapter is more about one of the people forever associated with the place rather than the house itself, for which there are many guides and books to peruse already.

A Gardener with a Difference

Joseph Paxton was one of the giants of Victorian engineering. He was born near London in 1803, the seventh son and last of nine children of William and Anne. His father was a tenant farmer. Joseph was poor and left school at fifteen to earn a living.

Paxton joined the Horticultural Society in London in 1823 and became a labourer at their garden in Chiswick. In 1826, aged 23, Paxton was offered a place at the gardens at Chatsworth House, by William Spencer the Duke of Devonshire. The Duke had seen Paxton's abilities when he was at his London property. Chiswick Villa, adjacent to the gardens.

At Chatsworth, Paxton fell in love with Sarah Bown, the niece of the housekeeper there, Mrs Gregory. They were married in February 1827 and moved to a cottage on the edge of the kitchen garden, near the river Derwent.

Paxton set to work on the extensive gardens, which had been somewhat neglected by the previous Duke. He built an orangery and then designed a 'stove' or glasshouse for growing vegetables in the kitchen gardens.

This glasshouse was a better and lighter design than any others built there, with a groove in the frames to hold the glass instead of using putty. Putty caused problems when it dried or disintegrated, allowing water and cold in. The frames to hold the glass were made of wood, as Paxton felt this was better, being easier to repair, more flexible and cheaper than iron.

Paxton was working hard during these first years and the Duke held him in high regard. He had Paxton work on a Pinetum, to show off varieties of conifer and also do much more landscaping work as well as a later arboretum with 1,670 species of tree.

On 19th October 1832, the young Princess (later Queen) Victoria visited Chatsworth. Paxton organised the waters in the park to be lit by multi coloured flares. Paxton's third daughter, born the same month, was named Victoria, in honour of this visit.

Look out for deer in the park

Glass Palaces

The Duke became fond of Paxton as a friend as well as an employer and they enjoyed sharing their love of gardening and plants. The Duke took Paxton to Paris and Versailles in 1834, the first of many travels which can not have been easy on Paxton's wife Sarah, left at Chatsworth waiting for news and letters and looking after the children alone.

Innovative works of glass

Paxton continued to work on the gardens, creating a rock garden (restored with a new viewpoint constructed in honour of Paxton's bicentenary in 2003) and worked on new designs for improving glasshouses, using a 'ridge and furrow' roof design.

The Conservative Wall, one of the glass structures built by Paxton

In early 1836, work began on one of Paxton's most famous buildings at Chatsworth, sadly now destroyed, (It was blown up in 1920 as it had suffered in the first world war), This was The Great Stove. This enormous conservatory (277ft/84m long,123ft/37.5m wide and 67ft/20.4m high) was heated with hot water rather than fires. A new road and underground tunnel for coal carts to feed the boilers were built. Railway tracks went into the stove basement. The building had cast iron columns and a ridge and furrow roof. Columns also acted as drainage so rainwater from the roof could be caught. This water was then heated. A maze is now on the same site.

At that time, a tax on glass by weight, meant that efficiency and economy to make things as light as possible were paramount. The ridge and furrow idea meant that when the sun was at a low angle it shone in more, getting more heat and when it was highest it hit the glass at a more oblique angle, so not too intensely. Paxton tried out this idea on small buildings, then built a huge orchid house. He made the front supporting columns hollow so they were also used as drainage from the roof. More and better glasshouses were needed for the exotic new arrivals Paxton collected. Many plants flowered for the first time in Britain at Chatsworth.

The trend for exotic plants had led intrepid gardeners to travel abroad on often dangerous adventures in search of new species. Paxton had bought a mini banana from Epsom and cultivated it. It was named Musa Cavendishi after the Duke in 1837. This plant is said to be the parent plant of all edible bananas now grown in Britain. Paxton also named an orchid after the Duke, Stanhopea Devoniensis. One of the plants brought back was named in Paxtion's honour too – Dendrobium Paxtonii.

The Great Stove conservatory that Paxton had built was ready to glaze in 1840. The glass was made in Birmingham, the biggest panes made at that time. Paxton invented a special wagon that ran along the roof to fit the glass as they went along- two men and a boy were in each wagon. Later this system was used at Crystal Palace. He adapted a grinding machine and attached it to a steam engine to make a groove in sash bars for adding glass more quickly. He was awarded a silver medal from the Society of Arts for the design.

In December 1843, Victoria and Albert visited. Thousands of oil lamps lit the gardens, illuminating the paths and the great conservatory, which the Royal couple entered without even getting out of their carriage it was so big.

A bust of Paxton at Sydenham Crystal Palace site

A Mighty Fountain

In 1844, The Duke heard his friend, Tsar Nicholas of Russia was visiting England and may come to Chatsworth. In his honour, Paxton designed the Emperor Fountain, right, capable of a height of 296 ft (90m), the highest gravity fed fountain in the world. A massive lake (nearly 8 acres) was built 400ft above to feed it, as well as a stream across the moors to feed the lake. The Tsar never saw it, however.

The Crystal Palace

A huge Victoria Amazonica lily was also a famous attraction at Chatsworth and flowered for the first time in this country there. Paxton built the lily a special tank which it outgrew twice and then a lily house. The lily leaves were big enough to stand his daughter Annie on. This lily and the rib pattern of the strong leaves were said to have inspired Paxton with ideas for his most famous project of all, The Crystal Palace.

The Great Exhibition was at Hyde Park, London, in 1851. A design was needed to house the exhibition and Paxton drew up hasty plans, winning the design commission. His fabulous creation, dubbed the Crystal Palace, had over 10 miles of exhibition space, was 1,848ft long, 408ft wide and 108ft high. It was designed so it could be easily dismantled and rebuilt, and required no mortar, stone or brick and no scaffolding. It was six times the size of St Paul's Cathedral and took just over 6 months to construct. As a result of the building's success, Paxton was given a knighthood.

Dinosaur models at the Sydenham Crystal Palace site

Though designed as a temporary structure, some people wanted to keep the Palace at the end of the exhibition, and use it as a winter garden. Eventually it was kept, but moved to Sydenham in Kent. At this new site, reopening in 1854, Queen Victoria came with much pomp. There were terraced gardens and also model dinosaurs. These were life size and the press were sent invites to dine inside an Iguanodon!.

The full and prolific life of Joseph Paxton came to an end on June 8 1865 at Rockhills, his home at the corner of the Sydenham Crystal Palace park. As well as designing and gardening, he had also found time to launch magazines, be involved in railway construction, lay out public parks and cemeteries, design buildings and be a Liberal MP for Coventry.

Paxton's body was taken back to his spiritual home of Chatsworth by special coach and he was buried near the duke at Edensor. His wife Sarah was buried with him six years later.

The Crystal Palace was for long after a fine spectacle, housing a museum and used for concerts. Finally this amazing structure was destroyed by fire in 1936. Some remains can still be seen at the site.

Some of Paxton's creations at Chatsworth can still be seen today of course, in the lovely gardens.

■ Chatsworth, Bakewell, Derbyshire, DE45 1PP
■ Telephone: (01246) 565300
■ www.chatsworth.org

Edensor Village

In 1838, the 6th Duke and Paxton worked on designs for houses at a new village of Edensor, in the grounds of Chatsworth. The village was reduced and re-modelled, with houses for the workers all but completed by 1842.

All houses had water and sewage drainage, a great example of social welfare. Lodges were designed for the park entrance, one Tudor and one Italianate in style, inspired by the Duke and Paxton's travels. The lodges still stand. Naboth's Vineyard is a house and garden where the old village was, positioned, over the road from its present site. It is thought the Duke left it there so the occupant was not disturbed by a move.

A winter scene of the Tudor style lodge

The most prominent building in the model village of Edensor is the church of St. Peter. An older church of St Peter was on the same site as the present church. The 6th Duke and Paxton worked on the village, but it was the 7th Duke who rebuilt the church. The Duke appointed George Gilbert Scott, a well known Victorian architect, to design it.

The plans were approved and in December 1864 work started. Scott designed most of the fittings too, including pulpit font, stalls, pews and ironwork. Stones from the older church on the site were saved to include in the new one. A tomb slab seen in the south porch is one found during church rebuilding work

The 12th century doorhead was re-used and has the characteristic Norman chevron pattern. The piscina, where the chalice is washed after communion, is from the old church too. The new church was completed and consecrated in 1870.

A Cavendish chapel was added to the new church as a private family chapel but also to fit in a huge Jacobean monument. The monument, now in a glass walled room, is for William, the 1st Earl of Devonshire who died in 1625 and also for Henry Cavendish who died in 1616. Both were sons of Bess of Hardwick. The monument also has a skeleton depicting Henry and in front of this is William in a shroud. The black marble slab over the effigies was once used as the altar as the monument originally stood at the east end of the chancel in the old church.

St. Peter's Church and a gargoyle from the south porch roof. Left is a fountain in the village. Top left is Naboth's Vineyard

The churchyard was later extended with a Cavendish Burial Ground, which contains memorials to most Dukes of Devonshire. The plot also contains a memorial to Kathleen, who was married to the Marquess of Hartington. She was the sister of President John Kennedy. Kennedy visited the grave in 1963, shortly before his assassination later that same year.

In the centre of the new churchyard is Sir Joseph Paxton's tomb, a table tomb.

The other graves in the churchyard are interesting too. A stone with a skull to the left of the church looking from the road has a poem 'Of stature great, of mind most just, here lies will Grumbold in the dust'

Left: The tomb of Sir Joseph Paxton and shields from it

Baslow

This village is near Chatsworth. Areas of the village known as Nether End and Goose Green are set around the entrance to Chatsworth Park. Near the river, as you walk into the park, is a view of some pretty thatched cottages. An iron Gate leads into Chatsworth. Near this gate is an old malthouse, with the blue plaque shown top right on it..

The oldest part of Baslow is Bridge End, with a lovely old church, dedicated to St. Anne. The clock on the 13th century tower is unusual because instead of numbers it says 'VICTORIA 1897'. This was an idea by a local man, Dr Wrench. He took over a medical practice after army service in the Crimean War. The clock inscription is to mark the diamond jubilee of Queen Victoria.

Thatched cottages and the gate leading into Chatsworth Park (left)

Close to the church is a 17th century three arched bridge. On this is a tiny tollhouse, like a miniature guard house. It is probably smaller because the level of the road has been raised. The toll-house is sometimes called Mary Brady's House, after a local beggar who once slept in there for shelter sometimes.

No lead or heavy millstones could be carried over the bridge and a fine had to be paid by those breaking the rule, hence the tollhouse.

Baslow Hall is in the part of the village named Over End. It was built for the Rev Jeremiah Stockdale, Baslow's vicar from 1859-1907. He died before it was finished and it became home to Sebastian de Ferranti, an electrical pioneer and inventor, who installed a fuel oil generator in 1925 to provide electricity.

Baslow once had a hydropathic hotel too. This provided health baths. Only the gateposts are left, but the nearby names Hydro Close and Hydro Cottage echo this now lost place, which was pulled down in 1936.

Stone Markers

Dr. Wrench has a monument in the churchyard. It is a short column topped with a sundial formed from a leaning cross.

There are other interesting graves to see, such as one in the shape of a coffin, with an hour glass on the top and carved iron carrying rings.

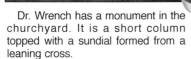

Wrench Monument and the stone coffin shaped tomb

On Baslow Edge stands the cross of the Wellington Monument, erected by Dr Wrench in 1866, to complement the Nelson Monument or Pole on Birchen Edge a mile away.

Above Baslow Edge stands a natural gritstone feature known as the Eagle Stone. It stands out for miles so was once used as an easy to spot meeting point for the packhorse trains. Prices were haggled over for such products as salt. This is why it has sometimes also been known as the Haggle Stone.

It also is said to have been used by local youths who had to climb it to show their prowess for marriage and that it turns around on some special mornings of the year at cock crow.

The Eagle Stone, Baslow Edge

Historic Edges

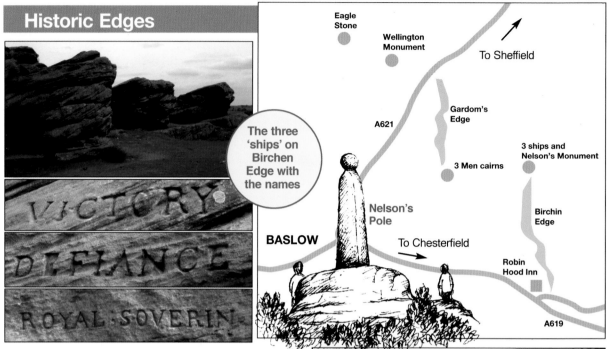

The three 'ships' on Birchen Edge with the names

From the Robin Hood Inn, on the Chesterfield Road, paths lead up to Birchen and Gardom's Edges. Three piles of stones, or cairns, not far from the inn are said to mark the graves of three men who left the inn after a few too many pints and got lost in a snow storm and died. These are marked as **E** on the diagram below.

On Birchen Edge can be seen Nelson's Pole, a monument to celebrate the Admiral's victory at Trafalgar in 1805. Nearby are three large rocks once called wainstones (because they looked like covered wagons (wain is another name for wagon, as in Constable's famous painting The HayWain). They were carved with the names of the ships which had taken a major role in the battle.

A view from Birchen Edge

Gardom's Edge

Evidence of the Peak District's prehistoric past have been discovered at Gardom's Edge. Here was a thriving community dating as far back as the Neolithic period around 5,000 - 4,000 years ago.

It is thought these people could have used the area for 'sky burials' or excarnation (where the flesh is removed from bodies by exposure to elements and scavenging birds).

From the Bronze Age, it would perhaps have been a more agricultural type of community,growing cereals and root crops.

Foundations of an entire round house have been uncovered, as well as pottery, flint tools and remains of a field system which has been cleared to plant in.

Rock art
The design right is carved into a boulder on Gardom's Edge. No one knows what it means, though it does look a little like some kind of map, maybe of huts, settlements and mounds.The boulder is now covered in a protective fibreglass replica to prevent the original carving getting damaged

Round House
Evidence was found of a round building during excavations. This was made of wood covered wattle and daub and with a thatch, turf or bracken roof. A fire would burn inside and an extended family would probably live in it. A human cremation, perhaps a family ancestor, had been buried under the floor

Stone bank enclosure
This enclosure seems to have been a special place, perhaps where people would gather for feasts and such. They would also lay corpses here to be picked clean by scavenging birds. The bones were then maybe used in rituals, or as protection, or put elsewhere

Cairns
Many of these rock piles scattered over the area were made almost by accident as the fields were cleared and rocks tossed aside. Some are more regular and may have had a more specific purpose

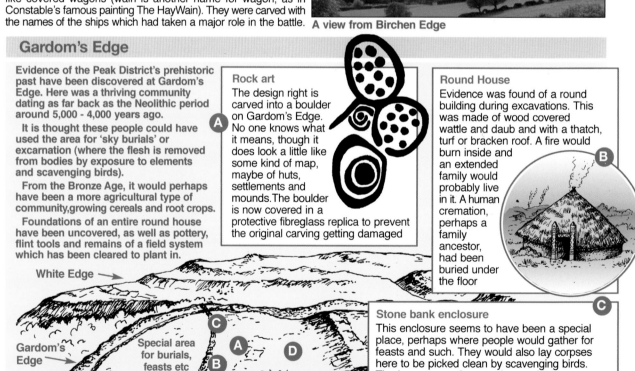

Darley Dale

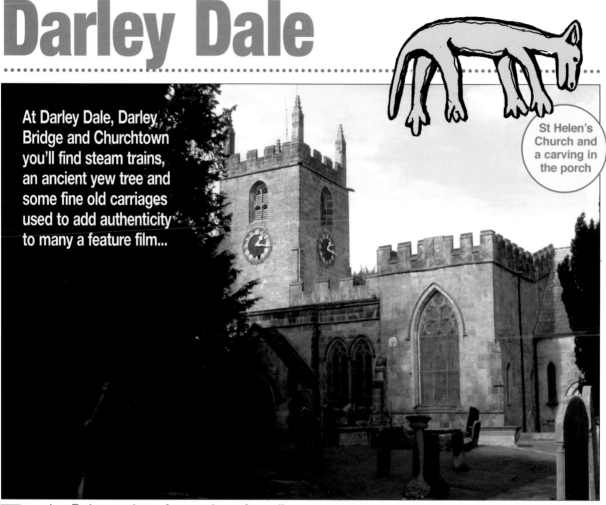

At Darley Dale, Darley Bridge and Churchtown you'll find steam trains, an ancient yew tree and some fine old carriages used to add authenticity to many a feature film...

St Helen's Church and a carving in the porch

D arley Dale consists of a number of small hamlets just off the A6, near Matlock. A scenic route there from Sheffield passes through Chatsworth Park, or you can travel part of the way by steam train.

An age-old tree

At first this area was known simply as Darley but it is thought the 'dale' may have been added by the railway company to make it sound more quaint and attract travellers, as this was once a railway village.

The churchyard of St Helen's has a wonderful and ancient yew tree, said to be well over 1000 years old. It certainly looks like it has been there forever, with its twisted boughs and huge trunk looking like something from a fairy wood.

The old yew tree at St. Helen's church-yard

The church dates mainly from the 14th century, but has earlier parts. The builders may well have rested for a jug of ale or two under the boughs of the growing yew.

To the right of the porch of the church are some old stone coffins. There are some interesting grave slabs and stones in the porch too. One is full of character and looks like a dog or a fox (shown above).

Stones and a sundial

The lovely church-yard and (right) the sundial

There is a badly eroded sun dial on the church wall. It has a gnomon (the part that casts the shadow) of iron scrollwork. It was erected by Rev. William Wray in the 18th century.

There are some fascinating grave stones and tombs around the churchyard, particularly near to the church where you can see ones with unusual designs such as a pentagram (5-pointed star, a Star of David (six pointed star), and what looks like weaving equipment such as loom and spinning wheel. Below are the stone coffins near the porch.

Some of the unusually decorated tombs and stones

GRACE BENET 1648

THOMAS SHORE 1710 AGED 2 YEAR

THOMAS IDE

Sir Joseph Whitworth (1803-1887)

Stockport born industrialist Sir Joseph Whitworth is one of the people buried in the churchyard at St Helen's. He was a great benefactor to the area after he bought nearby Stancliffe Hall.

Whitworth made his money with the manufacture of machine tools and armaments and also the introduction of the Whitworth screw thread in 1841, which standardised screw threads so all places could use the same size. The thread size he created became known as the British Standard Whitworth (BSW). It is now replaced by metric threads.

Other inventions included a knitting machine and a horse drawn street sweeping machine. The micrometer was also his idea. He had numerous exhibits at the great exhibition in London in 1851 and won many awards for his inventions.

During the Crimean War he was approached to mass produce Enfield rifles, but decided he could do better and developed the Whitworth Sharpshooter Rifle, as well as cannon. The rifle he created had a twisted hexagonal bore and he then shaped bullets to match this bore, patenting his designs in 1854.

It was from the generosity of Joseph Whitworth and his wife that the Whitworth Hospital, Whitworth Park and the Whitworth Institute (opened with the help of his wife in 1890, after his death) were founded. The Institute is now a much used community centre. During the years it had become run down, but the charity now running it received a grant in 1997 and a lot of work is going into restoring it.

■ The Joseph Whitworth Centre, Darley Dale, (01629) 733678

Red House Stables Working Carriage Museum

This is on Old Road, at Darley Dale. There is a fine collection of horse drawn carriages and associated equipment to be seen here and it is a working stables. The collection includes a Hansom Cab, Stage Coach and Royal Mail Coach. The Gay Gordon 1832 stagecoach, now at the stables, was once a familiar sight on the Great North Road between Edinburgh and London.

The unusual thing at Red House Stables is that all the carriages are still fully working and in use, often out on the road. Tours around the area in one of the old coaches are available by appointment – a splendid way to see the scenery.

The collection was established in 1946, by a Mr William Smith, who took great care over the authenticity and condition of the carriages, which are also available to hire for weddings. His daughter, Caroline Dale-Leech, now carries on the tradition.

The fine old coaches have been stars of many films, including Pride and Prejudice, Sense and Sensibility, Emma and Jane Eyre.

■ Red House Stables Working Carriage Museum,

Old Road, Darley Dale, Matlock, Derbyshire, DE4 2ER

■ Telephone (01629) 733 583

The author and other passengers in period costume climb aboard the Gay Gordon stagecoach on one of its outings from the Red House Stables Working Carriage Museum. In the bottom photo the post horn is being blown

Peak Rail

The railway was a big influence of Darley Dale's growth. The line running from Derby was opened as far as Rowsley by 1849 and extended to Manchester in 1867. Rowsley became a major railway depot and sidings. Later though, in 1968, the railway that ran between Matlock and Buxton, forming part of the Midland Railway's Manchester-London St Pancras line, was closed.

In 1975 it began to live again when enthusiasts formed Peak Rail, to work towards re-opening the line as far as Buxton, through Matlock. Darley Dale was Peak Rail's first station and has been restored and developed and now has a shop and cafe, with

steam trains running from here to Matlock, starting at their base in Rowsley. The Rowsley site, which became the Peak Village shopping outlet in 1999, is being developed now too. Parking at Peak Rail in Rowsley and getting a train into Matlock is a great way of beating traffic jams as well as supporting Peak Rail's endeavours.

There is usually a dining train running, as well as other themed and special events such as Santa Specials. Also available are steam experience courses, where you can learn to drive a train. Peak Rail are also often needing more volunteers to help them.

■ Peak Rail Plc, Matlock Station, Matlock, Derbyshire, DE4 3NA
Telephone: (01629) 580381

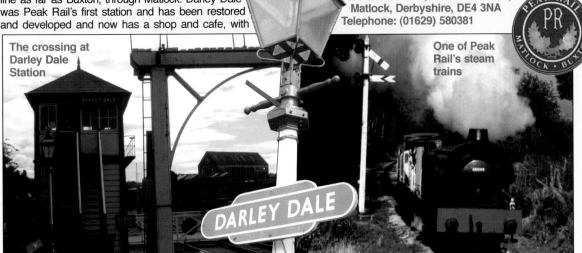

The crossing at Darley Dale Station

One of Peak Rail's steam trains

DARLEY DALE

Caudwell's Mill

At Rowsley is a listed, historic roller flour mill, powered by the water of the River Wye. A mill has stood on this site for at least 400 years...

The present mill to be seen in Rowsley is named after a man called John Caudwell (1827-91), who built it in 1874. It was run as a family business for over a hundred years. There were eight pairs of millstones, powered by a water wheel.

Powering the mill

John Caudwell demolished an older mill on the site at Rowsley and built his new one in 1874. It had two breast shot water wheels, one for the provender (animal feed) mill and one for the flour mill. Most of the equipment to be seen at the mill today dates from before 1914 and is still driven by belts and pulleys. The mill workings are fascinating, with water turbines and roller mills (which replaced the millstones used here until 1887). The machinery spreads over four floors, and still runs daily. The water turbines, turned by the flow of the river, took over from the waterwheels. The smaller turbine was installed in 1898 for the provender mill and the larger one in 1914 for the flour mill. The smaller one also generates the mill's electricity today.

Caudwell's Mill at Rowsley, with weir in the foreground

Right is Edward Caudwell, (1866-1941) the son of John, who leased the mill at Rowsley with his brothers Charles, Francis and Walter in 1887. Edward continued to modernise the mill and formed the firm of Edward Caudwell (Rowsley) Ltd.

Inside the mill

The mill acts like one huge machine and it shows how much work goes into producing the flour. There are strange sounding things such as worms, elevators, purifiers and agitators to be seen as you wind through the floors up to the top of the mill. Below is a brief description of a few of the items of equipment:

Elevators

This is one of the ways that the stock is moved around between floors. It consists of a rubberised canvas belt with small metal buckets attached along it. This is

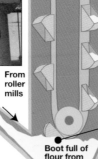

Out to sifter

At the top the bucket starts to go down again and tips upside down, throwing out flour down the shute

The buckets travel upwards

From roller mills

As each bucket gets to bottom it picks up flour

Boot full of flour from roller mills

housed in long wooden boxes. The endless belt passes over pulleys at the top and bottom of the elevator. The buckets pick up the stock from the large storage box (boot) at the bottom of the elevator and carry it up, tipping it out as it passes over the top pulley into a spout (wood or metal tube) and into another machine or part of the mill where it needs to go next. (see diagram).

Rollers

On the roller floor the grain can be turned into flour in just 15 minutes by the rollers it is fed through. Roller milling was a technique introduced to Britain in the early 1880s. It was a faster way of milling than millstones and produced a finer flour.

The millstones were used to mainly grind wholemeal flour. White flour was harder to produce and considered a luxury. With the arrival of these rollers white flour could be made more easily and brought the cost down. The rollers make the grain finer and finer until it is ready to be sent to the sifters two floors up.

Plansifters

These sifting machines are supported from the ceiling by flexible rattan canes that allow the machine to sway in small circles like it is doing a shimmy and sift the flour. The mesh sieves are enclosed in a wooden case. The white 'socks' are where the stock enters and leaves. The ones at the bottom make it look as if it has little legs dancing about like a sort of pantomime cow!

Plansifter and close up of the canes

Purifiers

These were for making white flour. They are long sieves that have air drawn up through them, lifting lighter particles and letting heavier unwanted particles fall back into the trays from where they are removed. White flour is no longer produced at Caudwell so these are no longer used.

Worm or Archimedean Screw

This is used to move stock horizontally in the mill, such as moving flour from the plansifters to the bagging plant. This type of screw is thought to have been invented in Syracuse by Archimedes around 200BC and was originally used to raise up water.

The worm consists of shaped metal blades that rotate on a shaft within a wooden box. As the blades turn they move the flour along within the box. Originally at the mill a worm would take up the untreated wheat, delivered by horse and cart, up to the mill's conditioning plant (now mostly removed) to clean it and remove stones etc. Now this is done before the wheat arrives and the wheat goes straight into clean wheat bins.

Agitator

These were used to bleach the flour to make it even whiter. Yellow pigment such as carotene, found in the 'endosperm' (see diagram next page), were bleached out by gas added to the flour in the agitator, which did just that and mixed them together. The agitator has a worm to move the flour into the gas. Flour is no longer bleached in this way.

Flour bagged and (bottom) for sale in the shop

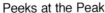

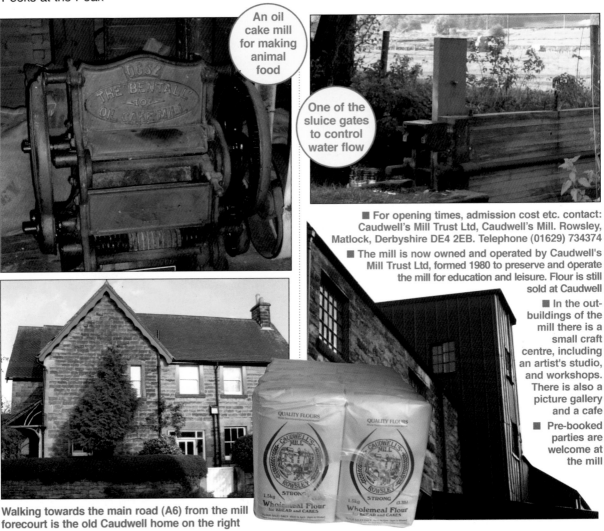

An oil cake mill for making animal food

One of the sluice gates to control water flow

■ For opening times, admission cost etc. contact: Caudwell's Mill Trust Ltd, Caudwell's Mill, Rowsley, Matlock, Derbyshire DE4 2EB. Telephone (01629) 734374

■ The mill is now owned and operated by Caudwell's Mill Trust Ltd, formed 1980 to preserve and operate the mill for education and leisure. Flour is still sold at Caudwell

■ In the out-buildings of the mill there is a small craft centre, including an artist's studio, and workshops. There is also a picture gallery and a cafe

■ Pre-booked parties are welcome at the mill

Walking towards the main road (A6) from the mill forecourt is the old Caudwell home on the right

An ancient process

Milling is the process which crushes the grain and opens it up to reveal the white endosperm inside. Early man used stones to do this, pounding the grain on a flat stone by hitting it with another. Later this developed into using specially shaped stones, called querns.

The saddle quern is one of the earlier types, when a stone shaped like a saddle held the grain and a second stone was rubbed backwards and forwards over it. A later type of quern developed was a rotary quern. This consisted of two stones one on top of the other. Grain was poured into the centre through a hole in the upper stone which was was turned with a handle to crush the grain. The crushed grain came out of another hole. Some of these rotary querns were known as beehive querns as they were a similar shape to a beehive. A saddle and a rotary quern can be seen at Caudwell's Mill.

In corn mills, pairs of circular stones are used to crush the grain. The upper stone, the runner, revolves whilst the lower stone, the bedstone, stays still. The surfaces of the stones have patterns cut into them which help tear and crush the grain. Examples of these stones can be seen left on the moors around the Peak District, as they were cut from the gritstone edges in this area.

Later in the industry, roller mills were developed, where the grain passes through iron rollers and sieving machines. These were fitted at Caudwell's Mill in 1885.

White and wholemeal

The wheat grain is a seed. The germ **(C)** is an embryo plant that will develop if left. Endosperm **(B)** is the food reserve the plant lives on until it develops a root system. Bran **(A)** is layers of skin that protect the seed. To make flour the grain must be ground to break it up into different parts. Types of flour vary according to the proportions of the three parts - bran, endosperm and wheatgerm, which are retained in the final product:

WHOLEMEAL = 100% extraction - all the parts are retained

WHITE FLOUR = 70-72% extraction, all bran and wheat extracted. A lot of the vitamins etc are also removed so this white flour is now not so popular. White bread has additives and vitamins put in it today by law

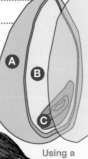

Using a rotary quern

Two querns that can be seen at Caudwell's Mill

Around Rowsley

Rowsley is an interesting place to wander. The village is in two parts, Great Rowsley and Little Rowsley. It stands at the confluence of two rivers, the Wye and the Derwent.

Look out in the village for an old toll house. Here was once the toll keeper for the 1759 Bakewell to Rowsley turnpike road, collecting the fees for using the road.

On the corner of Church Lane is an old drinking fountain, dating from 1841, set within a stone arch.

The Peacock Hotel is a very pretty and dominant building in the village. It was built in 1652 for a man called John Stevenson, an agent to the Manners family at nearby Haddon Hall. Later it became a farm and then an inn, in 1828. A grand stone peacock is atop the door. The peacock is the emblem of the Manners family. It has recently been acquired and revamped by Lord Edward Manners. Many actors from the film Pride & Prejudice, which starred Keira Knightly, stayed here in 2004 during filming at Haddon Hall.

The village church is worth a look. Dedicated to St Katherine and dating from 1855, it contains a fine tomb and effigy of Lady Catherine Manners and her twelve day old baby, who died in 1859. There is also a fragment of an old stone cross, labelled as a seventh century preaching cross found in the River Wye.

The drinking fountain

The boundary stone on the bridge

The tomb and cross fragment in the church

THIS FRAGMENT OF THE SEVENTH CENTURY ROWSLEY PREACHING CROSS WAS RECOVERED FROM THE RIVER WYE

The Rowsley bridge has a boundary stone marking the old boundary between Rowsley and Darley.

In 1849, Rowsley was the northern terminus for the Manchester, Buxton, Matlock and Midland Junction Railway. Many visitors came to Rowsley as a result of the railway, most of them on the way to see nearby Haddon Hall and Chatsworth House.

The Grouse and Claret Public House was once the Station Hotel. The station was designed by Joseph Paxton, gardener at Chatsworth and builder of Crystal Palace.

The section of the railway line to the northwest was over hills and an important coaling stage, so marshalling yard and engine sheds were built at Rowsley for the trains to refuel.

When the line was one of those closed in cuts by Beeching in 1967, this was not needed and was eventually turned into The Peak Village factory outlet shopping centre.

A local tragedy in song

On Saturday 9th February 1957, John Axon, a steam-locomotive driver, was making the down run on the line from Buxton. His fireman was called Ron Scanlon. The train was the 11.05am freight train from Buxton which weighed about 700-800 tons. They had just passed the 8.45 freight train from Rowsley to Edgley when disaster struck.

The steam brake pipe developed a fracture. The driving cab was filled with scalding steam and Axon was badly burned. The two men had to escape onto the steel step outside the cab and hang on. As the train was at this point going uphill, it was not too fast and so Axon told Ron to jump, which he did. Axon stayed hanging on, intending to alert the signalman at Doveholes of the danger of his train with no brakes working.

The train reached the crest of the hill and began to pick up speed, to more than 80 miles per hour. Axon had managed to alert the signalman, who passed on the danger to the other stations along the line and a train of passengers at Chapel en le Frith was moved out of the way to safety. It was too late for Axon to jump from the speeding train however. Seconds later he and the runaway train crashed into an empty freight train and John Axon was killed. He was posthumously awarded the George Cross for his bravery.

The act is also remembered in The Ballad of John Axon, which was commissioned in Autumn 1957. This was the first of a series of Radio Ballads commissioned by the BBC and was written by folk singer/songwriter Ewan McColl along with Charles Parker. It features the actual words of John Axon's wife, friends and comrades as well as steam train sounds and also songs based on the words spoken. The CD of this radio ballad is very moving and evocative of the times.

Matlock Bath

This is a place that feels like a trip to the seaside, with all the quaint charm of a Victorian spa town still clinging to the long popular spot, just next to the larger town of Matlock itself...

Matlock Bath became a centre for tourists because of the warm springs discovered there. It became even more popular in Victorian times, when wealthy people visited the Peak District as part of a nearer to home version of the Grand Tour.

A view of the hills and main parade at Matlock Bath

Little Switzerland

The high society of Victorian England were fond of Matlock Bath. It is still easy to picture them wandering by the river before partaking of the spa waters or tea on the terrace.

The spectacular scenery had Lord Byron liken the place to Switzerland and the cable car close by adds to this impression today. But well before these people, the benefits of the local spa were being developed. Daniel Defoe, on his own grand tour in 1724, went to Matlock and found that the site was in the midst of development even then..

"They are intending, as they tell us, to build a good house to entertain persons of quality, or such who would spend their money at it."

A new turnpike road was built in 1818, making Matlock Bath within more easy reach. The place had been a quiet hamlet, with agriculture and lead mining and quarrying creating employment. When the mills at nearby Cromford were built by Arkwright in the later part of the century, these created more jobs in the area. But it was really when man a called John Smedley based a centre for hydrotherapy (water treatment) in Matlock that the place really took off and became an 'in' place to visit. People began to make their home here, and houses were built clinging to the hillsides. peeking through the trees.

By 1849, the railway had made Matlock Bath an even more popular destination. More 'hydros' were built for the spa water treatment and events for tourists were created.

Venetian Nights were started as a celebration in honour of Queen Victoria's Diamond Jubilee. Boats were lit by candles and made a grand spectacle floating down the river. The Matlock Illuminations are still held every August to October.

The main road is split into two parts, South Parade and North Parade, which also makes it sound like it ought to be by the seaside. Over the River Derwent are the Lovers Walks, which can be reached by crossing the Jubilee Bridge.

A pretty pavilion at Matlock Bath

The Baths

Patients would 'take the waters' at Matlock Bath to cure rheumatic ailments and such, or improve digestion. Daniel Defoe took the waters of Matlock when he visited:

"...The bath is milk, or rather blood warm, very pleasant to go into and very sanative, especially for rheumatick pains, bruises &c."

One old Victorian Spa Bath is still to be seen. The Matlock Bath Hydro dates back to 1883. Some of the fine features remain, including the stone staircase where one can imagine the rustle of taffeta as Victorian ladies ascended. A stone drinking fountain is another feature from the bath's heyday.

The thermal pool itself is still in use and filled from the warm spring from the hillside. On a cold day, there is a haze of steam hanging on the pool's surface, as the huge girders that once held the roof arch overhead. The pool is now filled with a collection of large Mirror, Koi and Common Carp. As well as having the benefit of the spa waters that surely make them very healthy fish, they also get the luxury of being fed by visitors and suck up the food noisily with their huge mouths. The former consulting rooms are now home to an aquarium.

Next to the aquarium is a petrifying well display. The objects are from the original well which was once over the road. Spa waters playing on the objects deposit particles of calcium carbonate over the years and leave a layer of hard stone on them so they become bizarre sculptures (right).

Another display is the Hologram Gallery where 3D photographic images made by laser technology can be seen.

■ Matlock Bath Aquarium, 110 North Parade, Matlock Bath, Derbyshire DE4 3NS
■ Telephone: (01629) 583624

Cable car and castle

One of the most spectacular parts of Matlock Bath, the 'Heights of Abraham' gained the name at the time of the death of General Wolfe, in 1759. It was said the place looked like the Heights of Abraham in Quebec, which Wolfe scaled with his men to capture the area and Canada

PHOTOGRAPH: By kind permission of The Heights of Abraham

The tourist attraction at 'The Heights of Abraham' first opened to the public in 1780. Along with spectacular views, the Heights are also home to show caverns, dug out by 17th century lead miners. As trade in the lead mines wore out, the resourceful miners turned their hand to leading tourists to the area underground and into the cavern network. Once back above ground, vistors can explore the zig-zagging paths around the 60 acre woodland site as well as climb the Victorian Prospect Tower.

Visitors no longer have to climb the sides of the valley to reach the Heights as since 1984 it has had the country's first ever alpine style cable car system. In 2004 new observation cabins with bigger windows were introduced, which have easier access for wheelchairs and pushchairs.

The site also has shops, exhibitions, and a coffee shop.

■ The Heights of Abraham, Matlock Bath, Derbyshire, DE4 3PD ■ Telephone: (01629) 582365

■ Email info@heightsofabraham.co.uk

■ www.heightsofabraham.co.uk

A hidden gem

Just along from Matlock Bath, on the way to Matlock, a turning left from the main road leads up to a place that looks like a medieval palace, with a huge wall and turret, behind which is the little gem of St John The Baptist's Church.

This private chapel was built for a Mrs Harris in 1897 and is a lovely example of the Arts and Crafts Movement style.

It is a romantic place and almost feels as if there could be a knight on a vigil inside it. The place is normally kept locked and is in the care of the charity called the Friends of Friendless Churches, who have also done many repairs. It is possible to see inside if you make an appointment with the keyholder.

If you visit take care as there is a steep drop from the churchyard to the road.

■ The Friends of Friendless Churches,
St Ann's Vestry Hall, 2 Church Entry, London EC4V 5HB
■ Telephone: (020) 7236 3934
■ email: office@friendsoffriendlesschurches.org.uk
■ www.friendsoffriendlesschurches.org.uk

St. John the Baptist church

Riber Castle

Smedley, builder of the Hydrotherapy centre, also built Riber Castle. This is the castle that can be seen silhouetted on the skyline. He built it as a home for himself but died before it was finished. His wife and sons lived there. It later became a boys school, which closed in the 1930s and was then derelict until the 1960s when a small zoo/nature reserve was set up there. This closed in 2000.

The Old Pavilion

The pretty domed pavilion at Matlock Bath, once a health giving spa water centre, is now home to the Tourist Information Centre and the Peak District Mining Museum. This museum gives a fascinating glimpse of the history of lead mining, complete with models, equipment and recreated shafts to climb in. The shafts are used for practice by local rescue and fire teams. There is a shop with many good books about mining and industrial archaeology as well as gifts. See there also a real mine, Temple Mine, worked 1922-1940s..

■ Peak District Mining Museum and Temple Mine, The Pavilion, South Parade, Matlock Bath, Matlock, Derbyshire, DE4 3NR

■ Telephone: (01629) 583834
■ www.peakmines.co.uk
■ Email: mail@peakmines.co.uk

The old Pavilion at Matlock Bath

Lead Mining

Lead ore has been extracted in the Derbyshire area since at least the Roman occupation. Many 'pigs' of lead with Roman letters inscribed on them have been found. Most are marked LVTVD, an abbreviation of the name Lutudarum. This must have been a local place where the lead was from but no one now knows where this was. Galena is another name for lead ore.

LARVCONI·VERECVND·MEALLVIVD

Roman pig of lead found in Matlock. Note the last four letters LVTVD

The Romans called lead 'Plumbum'. They used it for many things, including water pipes and this is where our word 'plumber' comes from. The blocks were called pigs because they were made by one large pot of melted lead being run off into several small channels surrounding it and this was thought to look like a mother pig feeding baby pigs.

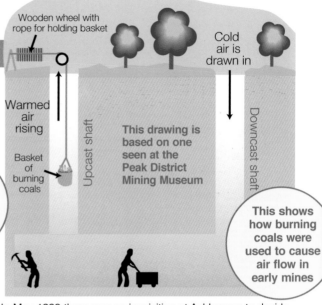

Wooden wheel with rope for holding basket

Warmed air rising

Cold air is drawn in

Upcast shaft

Downcast shaft

Basket of burning coals

This drawing is based on one seen at the Peak District Mining Museum

This shows how burning coals were used to cause air flow in early mines

Inhabitants of the 'dark regions'

The lead miners had a hard life in terrible conditions. Daniel Defoe gives a very evocative description of that 'subterranean creature' the miner in his book, Defoe's Tour Everyman Library Edition originally published in 1724:

'First, the man was a most uncouth spectacle; he was cloathed all in leather, had a cap of the same without brims, some tools in a little basket which he drew up with him.....For his person, he was lean as a skeleton, pale as a dead corps, his hair and beard a deep black, his flesh lank and, as we thought, something of the colour of the lead itself and being very tall and very lean he look'd like an inhabitant of the dark regions below and who was just ascended into the world of light.'

Defoe also saw a woman who lived in a cave:

"There was a large hollow cave, which the poor people by two curtains hang'd cross had parted into three rooms. On one side was the chimney and the man, or perhaps his father, being miners, had found means to work a shaft or funnel through the rock to carry the smoke out at the top.
....I asked what trade her husband was? She said, he worked in the lead mines. I asked her, how much he could earn a day there? she said if he had good luck he could earn about five pence."

Lead is of course poisonous and if land, water, animals or people were poisoned by it they were said to be 'bellanded.'

The lead that the miners dug was measured by volume, not by weight, and the volume was determined by a 'standard dish' the miners had to match. A standard dish was presented to miners by Henry VIII in 1513 and a resin cast replica of it can be seen at the Peak District Mining Museum. Twice each year these wooden dishes were brought to the local Moot Hall, home of the Barmote Court, which oversaw the mines, to be checked to see if they were the correct size. An old Barmote court at Wirksworth still stands, with an original dish kept there. Any miner who found a new lead vein had to give a dish of lead ore to the Barmaster at the Moot Hall to secure the mine for working. A portion of the lead ore found was given as a duty to the crown, a kind of tithe.

In May 1288 there was an inquisition at Ashbourne to decide the rights, customs etc of miners and try and get rules set. The meeting was called the 'Quo Warranto.' It became a kind of Bible for miners and was often quoted to clear up disputes. The Quo Warranto listed 14 rules the miners were supposed to live by. They were formed into a rhyming version by a man named Edward Manlove, in 1633. One rule he mentions is a gruesome one about punishment for stealing from another's mine;

"The thief that's taken fined twice shall be But the third time that he commits such theft, Shall have a Knife struck through his hand to th' shaft, Into the Stow and there till death shall stand."

Manlove also says that *"The Miners Terms are like to heathen Greek, both strange and uncouth, if you some would see."*

Left: Resin cast replica Standard dish of 1513 to be seen at the museum

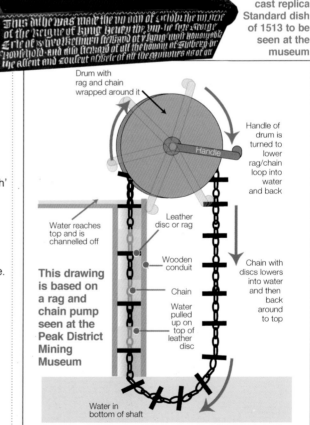

Drum with rag and chain wrapped around it

Handle of drum is turned to lower rag/chain loop into water and back

Handle

Leather disc or rag

Water reaches top and is channelled off

Wooden conduit

Chain

Water pulled up on top of leather disc

This drawing is based on a rag and chain pump seen at the Peak District Mining Museum

Chain with discs lowers into water and then back around to top

Water in bottom of shaft

The photo left shows a display at the Peak District Mining Museum, of a miner's equipment. The little bucket or 'kibble' to carry lead ore in can be seen in this old carving known as 't'owd man' from on the wall inside Wirksworth church

Above is a diagram of an early type of pump to remove water from mine workings. It was called a disc/rag and chain pump and consisted of leather discs or rags set on a chain at intervals, which drew up the water

Wirksworth

Wirksworth, four miles south of Matlock, is an ancient Saxon town, once the lead mining centre of the Peak. It has an age old church, housing a richly carved stone...

The church of St Mary the Virgin in Wirksworth was founded in 653AD, according to local tradition. The main fabric of the church is medieval, but there are some Saxon-age stones set within it's walls.

Ancient beginnings

At the time of the accepted founding of the church, in 653AD, Bakewell was the major religious centre and so was Repton, which still has a wonderful old Saxon crypt.

An old cross

Outside the Church of St. Mary the Virgin, is the shaft of a medieval cross, It is standing on what seems to be the base of a much older cross.

The slab

The 'Wirksworth Slab' or Wirksworth Stone is a Saxon grave-lid. Made of Millstone Grit, it was found in the chancel of the church during some rebuilding work in 1820. According to church records it was found two feet below the surface,

An 'angel' figure on the slab

with the carving face downwards. It was sited over a stone built vault that contained a large male skeleton.

Unproven tradition around the slab says that it was carved for Betti, the grandson of Penda, The King of Mercia in 653AD.

He is said to have come to Wirksworth to build a church. The slab is made from one large piece of stone, and the carving is of a high standard, with lots of drapery around the figures.

"there is no very great trade to this town but what relates to the lead works and to the subterranean wretches, who they call Peakrills, who work in the mines and who live around this town every way. The inhabitants are a rude boorish kind of people, but they are bold, daring and even desperate fellows in their search into the bowels of the earth."
An unflattering description of the town by Daniel Defoe in his tour of 1726 around Great Britain

The faces of each of the figures on the Wirksworth slab are very similar, elongated with pierced eyes. The hands and feet are carved in great detail, as are the wings of beings that look like angels, with similar lines to the drapery. The figures have quite 'pudding basin style', monkish haircuts..

The cross / crucifix has a lamb on it, often used as a symbol of the sacrifice of Christ. It is then quite likely that this stone was for a Christian person, because of this symbolism and the other possible biblical interpretations of other scenes on the stone, so it could have been for Betti.

The stone is now set into the north wall of the nave of the church, protected from the elements. Some parts of it have been lost and damaged over the years, but the carving was probably protected because it was buried.

Detail of the Wirksworth Slab

Christ figure?

The large picture is of the figure widely accepted to be Christ in most interpretations of the slab, including the one in the church guidebook (opposite).

Some archaeologist think the stone could be given an interpretation other than Christian, however. Left is a picture showing the overall shape of the slab.

The story on the slab

One interpretation is this widely accepted Christian one, found in the church

A. Christ washing the feet of his disciples

B. Crucifixion, showing a lamb and four evangelists

C. The blessed virgin being bourne for burial

D. Christ presented at the temple, the virgin on the right. Simeon holds the child in his arms.

E. Descent into hell. Christ is releasing man. in the form of a baby in swaddling clothes.

All but three souls, Cain Herod and Judas, are released. These three burn in a brazier

F. Christ in an oval panel holds a cross and is being taken to

heaven by four angels. The blessed virgin and Saint John are on either side below

G. The blessed virgin, seated, is greeted by the angel of the Annunciation, who carries in his left hand a scroll

H. A figure on the right, probably Saint Peter, stands in a boat (signifying the church). The Virgin Mary holds the Christ child on her left arm and he holds a scroll in his right hand, pointing to Peter with his left, to indicate how the word of God is to be transmitted. Behind Mary stand a man and a woman, who may be Saint Joseph and Saint Anne

The Church and some more carvings

The church

The church is made of red sandstone, with some limestone.

It stands in a serene green oasis, surrounded by Elizabethan 'Gells Armshouses' and also the Georgian former Grammar School.

An exterior view of the fine old church

T'owd Man

In the wall of the church is set an old stone with a perfectly charming naive style carving of a lead miner, carrying his little collecting bucket and his tool to dig. He is affectionately known as 'T'owd man' (the old man).

These carvings can also be seen inside the church

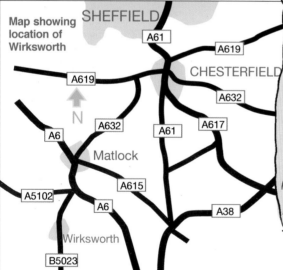

Map showing location of Wirksworth

SHEFFIELD
A61
A619
A619
CHESTERFIELD
A632
N
A632 A61 A617
A6
Matlock
A615
A5102
A6
A38
Wirksworth
B5023

An old tradition

Another old tradition is that of the annual ceremony of clypping (embracing) the church, when a circle of people surround the building, holding hands.

This takes place on the Sunday after the 8th September. A procession leaves Market Place and on reaching the church a hymn is sung. The people then encircle the church. A short service is held afterwards. It is not known when this custom, once more widespread, began, but at Wirksworth it was revived in 1921

Other attractions in Wirksworth

The town itself

Wirksworth is an interesting place, with many fine Georgian buildings still surviving. It was one of the 'barmotes' or administration boroughs of the medieval leadmining society.

DH Lawrence, who lived here for a year, is said to have called it the 'navel of England'.

There are many fine old buildings, many of which were restored under the "Wirksworth Project' of conservation in the 1980s, which won many awards.

The town also has the tradition of well dressing at the Spring Bank Holiday and a carnival and festival.

Some of the lovely old buildings in Wirksworth

Literary Connections

Wirksworth is also thought to be the 'Snowfield' of the Adam Bede novel and was the home of author George Eliot's aunt, Elizabeth Evans, said to be the model for the character of Dinah Bede.

The Barmote Court

Lead mining was carried out in Derbyshire for almost 2000 years, with the peak probably being around 1850. The ore, called Galena, was even quarried from under the town itself.

The mining is now gone, but many links remain, one of which is the old Barmote Court. In 1288 the 'Barmote Court of the Soke and Wapentake of Wirksworth' was formed, to settle any local lead mining disputes amongst other matters. The court location is at the Moot Hall on Chapel Lane. The Moot Hall was rebuilt in 1812 and the court still meets every year.

A measuring dish for ore, made around 1512, still hangs on the wall, as well as plaques depicting lead mining equipment.

The old Moot hall, home of the Barmote Court

An arresting place

Not far away from The Moot Hall is The Old Lock Up. This was built as a Magistrate's House in 1842. It served as a police station with cells for 100 years, until the 1950s. Now it is an unusual bed and breakfast, still retaining many of the old features, but a lot more home comforts!

Next to the Old Lock Up is a tiny mortuary chapel of rest, where the less timid guest can also spend a night or two bed and breakfasting.

The neighbours are quiet of course!.

An old cell door inside the Old Lock Up (right) and the old Chapel of Rest nearby (below)

The Heritage Centre

Wirksworth has a very good information source at the Heritage Centre, a former silk and velvet mill in Crown Yard, just off the Market Place.

Heritage Centre:

■ **Located at Crown Yard, Wirksworth, Derbyshire, DE4 4ET.**

■ **Telephone: 01629 825225**

Ring to check the opening times before visiting

Wirksworth Diary

Market Day: Tuesday

Early Closing: Wednesday for most, some open six days

Well Dressing: Spring Bank Holiday

Wirksworth Festival: Early September

Art and Architecture Trail: First week of the Festival

Some Peak wildlife

The Peak District is home to many species of bird, butterfly, plant and animal. This page shows just a few of the things you may see there...

Mountain Hare (Lepus timidus)

The only English population of this lovely creature is in the Peak District. These hares live higher up than Brown Hares and are also known as Blue Hares or White Hares, as in winter their coat turns white. Their ears are tipped black.

Mountain Hares are native to Britain unlike the Brown Hare (Lepus europaeus) and the rabbit, which are thought to have been introduced by the Romans. The Brown Hare does not turn white in winter.

Around March, the Mountain Hares can be conspicuous in their winter coat.

Hares live in a 'form' a shallow depression in grass. or sometimes make burrows. The young hares are called leverets.

Curlew

Curlews have an evocative and distinctive call – 'cur-lee', which is where the name comes from. Their long, downcurved beak is useful for digging up worms. They have long legs and webbed feet, for paddling in shallow water. They overwinter on mudflats and estuaries and return to the Peak District to breed and be found on upland pasture and heather moorlands, or near reservoirs.

The curlew, with a down turned beak

Lapwing

Stained glass depicting a lapwing

These are wading birds that return to the Peak District every summer to nest. They have a crest on their head and rounded wings. Locally they have another name – the 'pee-wit' as this is the call that they make. They nest in pasture fields and sometimes in burnt heather.

Grouse

You may see Red Grouse. Grouse have a distinctive 'go-back go-back' call. They live on the moorlands

Common lizard

Look out too for common lizards that may be basking on the rocks.

A male grouse

Common lizard

Butterflies

Speckled wood

Some of these beautiful creatures you could see include the brimstone, comma, common blue, orange tip, painted lady, peacock, red admiral, small heath, speckled wood and small tortoiseshell

Small tortoisehell

You may spot a Peacock butterfly on wild flowers

Some other birds

By rivers you may see heron, dipper and grey wagtail. Other places such as woodlands are home to redstart, pied flycatchers, wheatears, goldcrests, blackbird, black cap, bluetit, bullfinch, chaffinch, chiff chaff, goldfinch, greenfinch, nuthatch, robin, redwing, siskin, skylark, whitethroat and wren, plus many more to spot. On moorlands you may see short eared owl and ring ouzel.

Short eared owl

Grey wagtail

Skylark

Some plants to spot

Foxglove

Sundew

Cotton grass can be seen on wetter moorlands of the Peak, and looks like a soft white blanket when in flower in early July.

Heather gives a beautiful purple carpet in late summer. A less common plant you may spot is sundew, that likes boggy ground.

Wild flowers abound in the Peak and Derbyshire, including wood anenome, water avens, lesser celandine, ragwort, eyebright, scabious, self heal, rosebay willowherb, yarrow, yellow archangel, sweet cicely, hawthorn, foxglove, dog rose, St John's wort, red campion, white campion, cow parsley, coltsfoot, cowslip, birdsfoot trefoil (also known as bacon and eggs because of its colour, leadwort, early purple orchid, common vetch, to name but a few.

Wood anenome

Birdsfoot trefoil

Fly agaric

Fungi

Wood blewit

Look out for mushrooms and toadstools such as Fly agaric (this is poisonous), blewit, and cep. Bracket fungus grows on old trees.

And of course enjoy the beauty, shade, shelter and colour of all the trees you pass. Remember not to pick or damage flowers or disturb wildlife.

Words and wonders

Many literary people have been inspired, attracted or intruiged by The Peak over the centuries. Some described the wonders to be seen there in gushing words of praise. Daniel Defoe called it a 'howling wilderness'...

The 'Seven Wonders'

The Peak has long been a tourist destination, with many lengthy literary descriptions to its beauty. The area has been written about with varying degrees of detail and enthusiasm. Even in Elizabethan times the 'Wonders of the Peak' were already a subject worth discussion,

One of the first to describe the area in any detail and mention what he termed the 'wonders' was a man called Michael Drayton. Born (1563-1631). He was a poet and wrote in a style that earned him the name 'the English Ovid.'. In 1622 he published an extended edition of his long worked on book of songs called the *Poly–Olbion; A chorographical description of all the tracts, rivers, mountains, forests and other parts of the Renowned Isle of Great Britain'* which has a section about 'The Peake and its Seven Wonders' in song 26. Poly-Olbion translates as 'England which is blessed in many ways' and Drayton wanted people to go and appreciate the beauties of the country at a time when he felt there was 'nothing esteemed in this lunatic age but what is kept in cabinets' He says in the introduction that 'some people 'rather than take pain to search into ancient and noble things, chosest to remain in the thick fogs and mists of ignorance, as near the common lay-stall of a city, refusing to walk forth into the temple and field of the muses.'

Drayton's Peak wonders were; The Devil's Arse (Peak Cavern), Poole's Cavern and St Anne's well at Buxton, Eldon Hole,

Part of the cover image for Drayton's Poly-Olbion

'Pretty convenient for feeding sheep.'
A description of the Peak in Camden's Britannia

an ebbing and flowing well at Barmoor Clough, Mam Tor and Peak Forest.

Another work which describes the Peak appeared in 1586. It was by Londoner William Camden (1551-1623) and called 'Britannia.' The Britannia was written in Latin and first translated into English by a man called Holland in 1610 but there were also various later translations with additions. Camden described the area as:

'altogether rocky, rough, mountainous and consequently barren; yet rich in lead, iron and coal and pretty convenient for feeding sheep.' He tells the tale of the Devil's Arse *'very wide and gaping and having many apartments in it, wherein Gervasius Tilburiensis, either out of downright ignorance or a lying humour, tells us a shepherd saw a spacious country with small rivers running here and there in it and vast pools of standing water. yet from such stories as these, this Hole is look'd upon as one of the prodigies of England.'*

More musings about the 'Seven Wonders'

Another book about the 'wonders' of the Peak, was by the Enlightenment philosopher Thomas Hobbes (1588-1679), and called 'De Mirabilibus Pecci' - Being the Wonders of the Peak in Darbyshire'. The work was written in Latin around 1627 and first published in 1636.

When the book was translated into English in 1678 it included the original Latin with the English translation by 'a person of quality'. It became a great success. The title page held the dedication 'To the Noble Lord William, Earl of Devonshire Concerning the Wonders of the Peak.' (Hobbes was the tutor of the Cavendish family of Chatsworth and is buried in Ault Hucknall church). The title page also has a poem that begins:

"On th'English Alps, where Darbies Peak doth rise High up in Hills, that Emulate the Skies"

so any people visiting would indeed have expected big peaks.

At the end are the words:*"To Buxton we return, and dining quick, Our horse are brought and we through clouds convey'd by Sheldon...and Ashford...To Chatsworth famed, where the swift Derwin* (Derwent) *runs."*

The wonders listed are like those of Drayton: Mam Tor, ebbing and flowing well, Eldon Hole, St Anne's Well, Poole's Cavern, Peak Caven. The one that's different is Chatsworth - he even put it first on the list- maybe he was just trying to please his employer.

A little later, in 1681, Charles Cotton (1630-1687) produced his version of the highlights of the area, 'The Wonders of the Peak'.

Cotton was an English writer and angler, friend of Isaak Walton. He wrote the second part of Walton's celebrated book, 'The Compleat Angler.

Cotton's wonders were the same as those which Hobbes had listed, including Chatsworth. Thought he wasn't quite so glowing about Chatsworth and thought that it was *'built in a barren vale...nothing but winter ten months of the year.'*

"..through clouds convey'd by...Ashford"
Thomas Hobbes

A Howling Wilderness...

In 1724-1726, the writer Daniel Defoe (author of Robinson Crusoe and A Journal of The Plague Years) went and did his own exploration of the 'Wonders of the Peak', as he was researching his book 'A Tour Through the Whole Island of Great Britain.' He wasn't so impressed with most of the wonders described by Hobbes and Cotton:

"And now I am come to this wonderful place the Peak, where you will expect I should do as some others have, (I think foolishly) done before me, viz. tell you strange long stories of wonders as (I must say) they are most weakly call'd; and that you may not think me arrogant in censuring so many wise men, who have wrote of these wonders, as if they were all fools,....I cannot but, after wondering at their making wonders of them, desire you, my friend, to travel with me through this howling wilderness in your imagination and you shall soon find all that is wonderful about it..."

Defoe's work took more notice of the hardships the people living there had in their day to day existence, such as the terrible lot of the lead miners, instead of just romancing about the beautiful scenery.

As mentioned, Defoe was very dismissive about the so-called 'wonders'. Right are some of his comments.

On Pooles Cavern: *'Cotton and Hobbes are most ridiculously witty upon it. Poole's Chair, Flitches of Bacon and the like, are nothing but ordinary stones and little resemble the things they are said to represent'.*

He only seemed impressed by Eldon Hole and Chatsworth:
On Eldon Hole: *'which we may justly call a wonder'* *'a frightful chasm'*

On Chatsworth: *'Indeed a most glorious and magnificent house. If there is any wonder in Chatsworth it is that any man who had a genius suitable to so magnificent a design, who could lay out the plan for such a house and had a fund to support the charge, would build it in such a place where the mountains insult the clouds, intercept the sun and would threaten, were earthquakes frequent here, to bury the very towns, much more the house, in their ruins'*

"A most glorious house"
Daniel Defoe

Some other writers connected with The Peak District & Derbyshire

Ranulph Higden

He was a 14th century writer, a Benedictine monk at Chester, who produced a book called the 'Polychronicon' a history book of the times up to his own and much enjoyed then.It was translated into English from Latin

Celia Fiennes

Celia Fiennes (1662-1741) did a grand tour of England from 1685-1703, a pretty impressive thing for the conventions of the time as she went alone except for two servants. She wrote a journal about her travels, which was discovered after her death and published under the title' Through England on a Side Saddle.'

She wrote that Derbyshire was *'full of steep hills... and the miles long, you see neither hedge nor tree but only low drye stone walls.'*

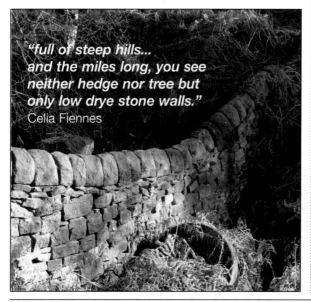

"full of steep hills... and the miles long, you see neither hedge nor tree but only low drye stone walls."
Celia Fiennes

Charlotte Bronte

As mentioned in the chapter on Hathersage, Charlotte Bronte (1816-1855), stayed in the rectory there when visiting her friend Ellen Nussey, whose brother Henry was the vicar. Her novel Jane Eyre is inspired by the history and buildings of the area.
Thornfield Hall, Mr Rochester's home, is very likely to have been based on North Lees Hall, on the outskirts of Hathersage, which fits her description.

George Eliot

This was the pen name for Mary Ann Evans, the author of Adam Bede and Middlemarch, among others.
She had relatives in Wirksworth whom she stayed with and it is generally believed that Wirksworth is the setting for Adam Bede, with the name of Derbyshire becoming Stoneyshire.

D H Lawrence

He lived for several years at Middleton-by-Wirksworth. The film of his book The Virgin and The Gypsy used Youlgrave and Beeley Moor as locations.

Anna Seward

Anna was a poet born at Eyam rectory in 1747. Thomas Seward, her father, later became a canon at Lichfield Cathedral and she moved there in 1757. Thomas was a friend of Erasmus Darwin, grandfather of the famous and controversial Charles. Anna wrote romantic poetry from an early age and had a collection of her poetry edited by Sir Walter Scott and published in 1810. She was known as the 'Swan of Lichfield.' She also wrote Dr Darwin's memoirs.

Edith Sitwell

This twentieth century eccentric writer and her family came from Renishaw and the lovely hall there is the family home still. There is an interesting museum about them at the hall.

Some other writers connected with The Peak District & Derbyshire

Sir Walter Scott

He wrote a book called Peveril of the Peak (and also one called Ivanhoe which is set around Conisborough).

Edward Bradbury

He produced a book called 'All About Derbyshire' in 1884. Chapters include 'A Cruise Round Castleton', where he waxes lyrical about Blue John.

Lord Byron

The famous poet 'mad bad and dangerous to know' Lord Byron visited Derbyshire and ventured down Peak Cavern. He was impressed by the area, being moved to write:

'There are things in Derbyshire as noble as in Greece or Switzerland'

Mary (Wollstonecraft) Shelley

Writer and also the wife of the poet Shelley, she created the famous gothic horror novel 'Frankenstein', which has spawned a good many creaky and enjoyable horror films over the decades. She mentions Matlock in Frankenstein, in chapter 19:

'We left Oxford with regret and proceeded to Matlock, which was our next place of rest. The country in the neighbourhood of this village resembled. to a greater degree, the scenery of Switzerland....We visited the wondrous cave and the little cabinets of natural history"

Maybe she had visited or maybe Byron told her about the 'Swiss' nature of the area when she and her husband were staying with him at the Italian villa where they first talked of horror tales and decided to see who could come up with the best one.

Sir Arthur Conan Doyle

The creator of Sherlock Holmes was no stranger to the Peak District, visiting probably when he was once living in Sheffield. He tells a horror tale of The Terror of Blue John Gap, about a monster living deep in the cavern there (see the chapter on Castleton).

Ben Jonson

The 17th century poet wrote about the Devil's Arse and his version of how it got that name in his epic masque 'The Gypsies Metamorphos'd. (see the chapter on Castleton)

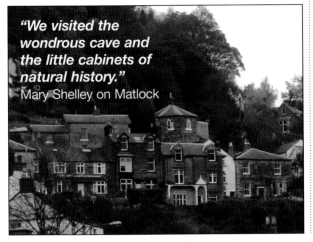

"We visited the wondrous cave and the little cabinets of natural history."
Mary Shelley on Matlock

"Well doctor, you're not afraid anyhow...of the terror that lives in the Blue John Cave..."
Sir Arthur Conan Doyle

Jane Austen

It is widely believed, though not proven, and disputed by some, that Jane Austen (1775-1817) visited Derbyshire. Also that Pride and Prejudice was partly written in Bakewell, (with the name changed to Lambton in the book).
Some say she stayed at the Rutland Arms there and that nearby Chatsworth House was the inspiration for Mr D'Arcy's posh pad, Pemberley. Pemberley certainly sounds like Chatsworth from the description in the book, though it could fit the description of other places too:

"They gradually ascended for half-a-mile and then found themselves at the top of a considerable eminence, where the wood ceased and the eye was instantly caught by Pemberley House, situated on the opposite side of a valley, into which the road with some abruptness wound. It was a large, handsome stone building, standing well on rising ground and backed by a ridge of high woody hills; and in front, a stream of some natural importance..."

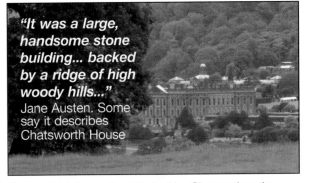

"It was a large, handsome stone building... backed by a ridge of high woody hills..."
Jane Austen. Some say it describes Chatsworth House

Jane certainly knew about Derbyshire. She mentions the place and indeed Chatsworth, earlier in the book...

"They were obliged to give up the Lakes, and substitute a more contracted tour and...were to go no further northwards than Derbyshire. In that county there was enough to be seen to occupy the chief of their three weeks...
"The town where she had formerly passed some years of her life, and where they were now to spend a few days, was probably as great an object of her curiosity as all the celebrated beauties of Matlock, Chatsworth, Dovedale, or the Peak." Chapter 43

So maybe she did visit, or perhaps she didn't...but based her descriptions of the towns and Pemberley on another place. Or she may have just listened to / read of the words of others who had visited the Peak and Chatsworth.
www.pemberley.com is a website with lots of information about Austen and her works.

Some other writers connected with The Peak District & Derbyshire

William Wordsworth

The famous poet was impressed with Chatsworth House and wrote a poem about it:

'Chatsworth! Thy stately mansion and the pride of thy domain, Strange contrast do present to house and home in many a craggy rent of the wild Peak."

John Ruskin

The famous Victorian novelist and critic often visited Derbyshire and was a great objector to the railway line through Monsal Dale, and hated the viaduct which was built there. He said the railway meant that

"every fool in Buxton can be in Bakewell in half an hour and every fool in Bakewell in Buxton."

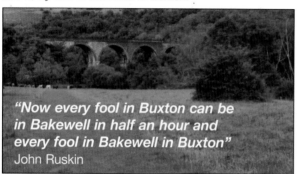

"Now every fool in Buxton can be in Bakewell in half an hour and every fool in Bakewell in Buxton"
John Ruskin

Some film and TV productions that used the Peak District as a location

Films:

The Princess Bride (with a giant fighting on Stanage Edge, and Haddon Hall as a royal palace)

Jane Eyre by Franco Zefferelli used Haddon Hall (as Rochester's house), Stanage Edge, Wingfield Manor (as the ruins of Mr Rochester's house), and also used period carriages from Red House Stables at Darley Dale

The Virgin and the Gypsy This film of the book by D H Lawrence uses Wirksworth

Television:

Chronices of Narnia (Peak Cavern, Chatsworth and Haddon Hall)

Peak Practice was filmed on location in Derbyshire, including Crich and Wirksworth.

It also used Holloway, near Matlock. as a location. This was once home to Florence Nightingale. It is now a conservation village. The 1853 chapel there is now a holiday cottage.

Stig of the Dump BBC adaptation used Darley Dale amongst other places

www.yorkshireonscreen.com
Has details of locations used in film and television productions

A locally inspired opera...

Sir Arthur Sullivan (1842-1900) was an English composer best known for his operatic collaborations with the words of W.S. Gilbert. Sullivan was born in Lambeth, London and produced many musical offerings still often performed today. One of his works was called Haddon Hall, which he wrote in 1892, and was inspired by the romantic elopement tale of Dorothy Vernon of Haddon Hall, near Bakewell, Derbyshire. It is a light opera in three acts, with music by Sullivan and a libretto by a man called Sydney Grundy.

Haddon Hall was premiered at the Savoy Theatre, London, on September 4, 1892 and had a run of 204 performances. The story is different to what is widely accepted as the tale of the elopement of Dorothy and her disapproved of lover, John Manners, in 1563. As Grundy notes in the libretto:

"The clock of Time has been put forward a century and other liberties have been taken with history."

Many words allude to Haddon Hall:

ACT 1- The Lovers. Scene - The Terrace.
"The green old turrets, all ivy thatch.
Above the cedars that girdle them rise"...
"Ye stately homes of England
So simple yet so grand;
Long may ye stand and flourish,
Types of our English land."

The change in date to 1660, just before the Restoration of the Monarchy, allowed Grundy to add humour by picking on the Puritans and their rather dour and funless view of life as the butt of jokes. He has the Puritans singing a chorus making fun of their disapproval:

"Down with Princes, down with peoples!
Down with churches, down with steeples!
Down with love and down with marriage!
Down with all who keep a carriage!
Down with lord and down with lady -
Up with everything that's shady!"

Other differences are that Dorothy is an only daughter when really she had a sister and there is a very strange Scottish character called the McCrankie for comic relief, not one to get past any racial stereotyping restrictions!:

"My name is McCrankie, I am lean lang an' lanky. I'm a Moody an' a Sankey, Wound upon' a Scottish reel!...
I don't object tae whiskey, but I say a' songs are risky, an I think a' dances frisky."

The actual elopement scene is very romantic and worthy of any novel, with the characters singing:

"The horses are waiting - And ready am I!
The storm is abating - Come, love, let us fly!
Oh, grant me one moment! The horses are waiting! -
Dear Haddon, good-bye! Come, love, let us fly!"

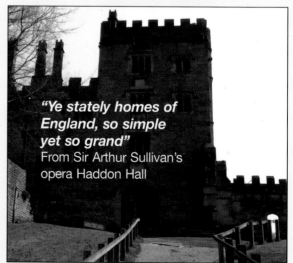

"Ye stately homes of England, so simple yet so grand"
From Sir Arthur Sullivan's opera Haddon Hall

Bibliography/further reading

A Thing In Disguise, The Visionary Life of Joseph Paxton
Kate Colquhoun (Harper Perennial) ISBN 0 00 714354 0
Excellent, well written and fascinating biography of this
amazingly clever and prolific man

Paxton's Palace
Anthony Bird (Cassell)   ISBN 0 394 29498 5
A book about Joseph Paxton and the Crystal palace, sadly
out of print at time of writing. A very detailed and technical
account, but well worth trying to trace a copy in second
hand shops etc.

Customs of the Peak District and Derbyshire
John N Merrill   ISBN 0 907496 34 2
More than you'd think but some may be disappearing fast, so
good to have a look and remember them to keep them alive

Bakewell. The Ancient Capital of the Peak.
Trevor Brighton   ISBN 1- 84114 - 4193
Very interesting, detailed and knowledgeable history of
Bakewell, with photos maps and the latest research and
discoveries, from the President of Bakewell and District
Historical Society

Mrs Ann Greaves & The Bakewell Pudding
Trevor Brighton A booklet from the Old House Museum,
Bakewell, dispelling many of the long told tales about this
famous delicacy

Jonson's Masque of the Gypsies:
An attempt at reconstruction by W.W.Greg.
Published in 1952 in London for the British Academy by
University Press Oxford. It shows the different versions of Ben
Jonson's masque about the Gypsies feast in Peak Cavern,
Castleton, The Gypsies Metamorphos'd. It is available to read
in the Arts and Social Sciences Library, Sheffield

The Seven Blunders of the Peak,
Some Derbyshire Legends Reassessed
Edited by Brian Robinson
ISBN 0-907758-77-0
Tales well known in Derbyshire, such as the Eyam Plague,
Little John's grave and Blue John are covered in a new light

Plagues -Their origin, history and future
Christopher Willis
ISBN 0-00-255611-1
Accounts of the different nasty diseases that afflict us and
their history, discovery etc. Easy to read and enjoyable
despite sounding depressing!

The Black Death - A Biological Reappraisal
Graham Twigg (Batsford Academic and Educational, London)

The Biology of Plague -
Evidence from Historical Populations
Susan Scott and Christopher J Duncan
(Cambridge University Press)

Murder and Mystery in the Peak
Roly Smith ISBN 1-84114-369-3
Entertaining and interesting accounts of spooky and deadly
goings on over the years

A view on the way up to Birchen Edge

Derbyshire Blue John
Trevor D. Ford ISBN 1 87377519 9
Extremely detailed and informative book about the gem

Rocky Rambles in the Peak District
Fred Broadhurst looks at the geology beneath your feet
ISBN 1-8508-750-7

Family Walks in the Peak District and South Yorkshire
John Spenser and Ann Beedham did this illustrated Star
Newspaper book of 52 routes graded for ease
ISBN 1 - 85284 257 1

Derbyshire Churchyards
Joyce Critchlow ISBN 0 946404 28 3
Some details to spot, such as sundials and crosses

Prehistory in the Peak
Mark Edmonds and Tim Seaborne ISBN 0 7524 1483 6
Very detailed with very good grid refs,
geographic/historical/technical detail in profusion

Archaeology Walks in The Peak District:
Ali Cooper ISBN 1 850 58 7078
A good way to make history come to life and enjoy a day out

Derbyshire origins A field guide to archeological sites in
North Derbyshire from Sheffield City Museums

Celtic Derbyshire
Peter Naylor ISBN 0 946 404 10 0

Curiosities of the Peak District
Frank Rodgers ISBN 0 903485 47 8
Lots of things to go out and spot that you may have missed

Hidden Derbyshire
Richard Stone ISBN 1 85306 715 6
Some lesser known places to visit and explore

Bibliography/further reading

Supernatural Peak District
David Clarke   ISBN 0 7090 6512 4
Journalist and folklorist David Clarke looks at tales of boggarts, black dogs, ghosts etc and talks to people about the strange goings on in the Peak

The Lunar Men - The friends who made the future
Jenny Uglow   ISBN 0 571 21 610 2
Telling of Erasmus Darwin and the other intellectuals who formed this fascinating society

How it all Began in Yorkshire Volume 2
Maurice Baren ISBN 1 855 68 183 8
Easy to read and colourful book tracing the beginnings of many famous names, including Fox Umbrellas, Comet, Thorntons and Bassett

Camden's Britannia:
Wordy late 16th century text that describes the Peak, but fascinating to read

A Tour Through England and Wales: Daniel Defoe
(Everyman Library) Originally Published 1724
A wonderful insight to Defoe's contemporary, sometimes moving, sometimes scathing impressions of the Peak and its people

The Terror of Blue John Gap: Arthur Conan Doyle
A gothic horror tale of a monster in the caverns from the creator of Sherlock Holmes, probably inspired by his visits to Castleton when he was living in Sheffield

Jane Eyre By Charlotte Bronte
A popular classic romance of Jane and the enigmatic Mr Rochester, that has Hathersage and surrounds as a most likely inspiration for the setting. Jane stayed at the vicarage at Hathersage when visiting her friend there

Walls Across the Valley
Brian Robinson
ISBN 0 90 7758 57 6
Now out of print but still in the public library in Sheffield. A fascinating look at the impounding of the reservoirs in the Upper Derwent Valley. Lots of technical details of the dam building, plus wonderful photographs. Some of Professor Robinson's family lived and worked at Birchinlee and this book has many photographs of the village life

Memories of Tin Town Professor Brian Robinson
JW Northend Ltd. ISBN 0 901100 40 4
Howden and Derwent Professor Brian Robinson
JW Northend Ltd. ISBN 0 901100 49 8
These two books are two smaller versions of the information, stories and photographs in the one above, still available.

The Mystery of Carl Wark: Peak District fortress or folly?
Mick Savage ISBN 1 9015 8706 1
Discussion about the enigmatic feature that may or may not be a hill fort

The Iron Age Hillforts of England
Geoffrey Williams   ISBN 1 897817 07 X
Scholarly text full of detail, with Derbyshire's MamTor and Carl Wark included

Collins Gem Guide to Wild Flowers
Marjorie Blamey and Richard Fitter
ISBN 0 00 458 801 0 and
Collins Gem Guide to Butterflies and Moths
Brian Hargreaves and Michael Chinery
ISBN 0 00 458 808 8
Ideal for sticking in the pocket when wandering around countryside, graveyards etc.

Notable Churches of Derbyshire
Robert Innes Smith
ISBN 0 85 100 072

The Anglo Saxon Chronicles

Peveril of the Peak, By Sir Walter Scott, published in 1823
Story of Sir Geoffrey Peveril, an old cavalier and Major Bridgenorth, a Puritan. Tales of Popish plots and unfair imprisonment

All About Derbyshire
by Edward Bradbury, 1884. Simpkin Mashall and Co.
Flowery text as he travels around with his companion Kalmat an rambles on beautifully about blue john etc

A Guide to Norman sites in Britain
Nigel and Mary Kerr   ISBN 0 586 08445 2
Easy to read and with photographs. The Derbyshire/Peak ones are Peveril Castle, Melbourne and Youlgreave font

England's Thousand Best Churches
Simon Jenkins
ISBN 0-713-99281-6
Derbyshire/Peak/local ones included are Ashbourne, Ashover, Ault Hucknall, Bakewell, Chesterfield, Steetley, Tideswell Wirksworth and Youlgreave

Roman Derbyshire
John J Anderson
Small book about the Roman sites in the area

The Peak District - Landscapes through time
John Barnatt and Ken Smith ISBN 0 77134 7529 3

Arbor Low- A Guide to the Monuments
Peak National Park Publications
ISBN 0 9075 43 74 X

Vestiges of the Antiquities of Derbyshire
Thomas Bateman, 1848

Padley Chapel
Barbara M.
Smith
ISBN
086384
2089

Peveril Castle, Castleton

Useful web addresses and telephone numbers

www.english-heritage.org.uk

www.nationaltrust.org.uk

www.americancivilwar.org.uk
A website that has details of the Whitworth Sharpshooter Rifle, as used in the Civil War and developed by Whitworth, who lived at Darley Dale.

www.learningcurve.gov.uk
Lots of history notes and information designed for schools and reference. Has details of engineers, textile industry etc

www.pioneers.historians.co.uk
A website with details of many great inventors and engineers, such as Whitworth and Paxton

www.peakdistrictonline.co.uk
Very comprehensive- accommodation to customs, villages, weather, cycling. cricket, childrens activities etc etc

www.peakdistrict-nationalpark.info
All aspects of the peak in this informative site, including geology, wildlife,people, and a virtual guided walk.

On line search facility provides access to reports on biodiversity, archaeology etc.

www.visitderbyshire.co.uk
History, information, famous people,market days, directions,

www.picturethepast.org.uk
A site showing historic photos of Derby, Derbyshire, Nottinghamshire and where you can purchase them on line.
Many photos are over 100 years old

www.haddonhall.co.uk
The hall's own website

www.nationalstonecentre.org.uk
Site about the centre near Wirksworth

www.chatsworth.org
The Chatsworth website

www.heights-of-abraham.co.uk
The attraction at Matlock

www.peakmines.co.uk
Website of the Peak District Mining Museum. Matlock Bath

www.caudwellsmill.museum.com
Informative site about this mill at Rowsley

www.eyamhall.com
About the lovely hall and craft centre

www.peakrail.co.uk
The preserved steam railway from Rowsley to Matlock

Peak District Rangers
■ email: rangers@peakdistrict.gov.uk

Peak District National Park Authority
Aldern House
Baslow Road Bakewell,
DE45 1AE
(01629) 816200

www.peak district.gov.uk
They work towards sustainable development of the Peak District.

■ **Wirksworth Heritage Centre**
(0114) 01629 825225

www.showcaves.com
Features the caverns at Castleton

■ **Peak Cavern**
(01433) 620285
www.devilsarse.com

■ **Speedwell Cavern**
(01433) 620512
www.speewdwellcavern.co.uk

■ **Treak Cliff Cavern**
(01433) 620571
www, bluejohnstone.com

■ **Blue John Cavern**
(01433) 620638
www, bluejohn-cavern.co.uk

■ **Bakewell Old House Museum**
(01629) 813642
www.oldhousdemuseum.org.uk

■ **Eyam Museum**
(01433) 631371
www.eyam.org.uk

■ **Caudwell's Mill**
(01629) 734374
www.caudwell'smillmuseum.com

■ **Fairholmes Visitor Centre**
(01433) 650953
E.mail: cyclehire@peakdistrict.gov.uk

TOURIST INFORMATION CENTRES

■ **Bakewell**
Tel: (0870) 4447275
Email: bakewell@peakdistrict.gov.uk

■ **Castleton**
(01433) 620679
Email: tourism@peakdistrict.gov.uk

■ **Matlock**
(01629) 583388
Email: matlockinfo@derbyshiredales.gov.uk

■ **Matlock Bath**
(01629) 55082
Email: matlockbathinfo@derbyshiredales.gov.uk

Thanks to:

- Professor Brian Robinson
- Tony Marsden, Peak Cavern
- John Harrison, Speedwell Cavern
- Vicky Turner and Treak Cliff Cavern
- Peter Harrison
- Robin Hall, Peak District Mining Museum, Matlock Bath
- Chatsworth
- Phillip Eastwood, Grindleford Cafe
- Trevor Brighton
- Brenda Roddis, Peak Park Ranger
- Haddon Hall
- Chris Thorpe
- Graeme Walker, Caudwell's Mill
- The National Stone Centre

- The Heights of Abraham, Matlock
- The Aquarium, Matlock Bath
- Pete Barnatt
- Don Hughes, Wirksworth
- Barbara M Smith
- Samantha Chidlow, National Trust
- Rev. Tony Bell, Ault Hucknall
- Jane Bownes, Bradwell's Ice Cream
- Red House Working Carriage Museum
- Jackie and Peak Rail
- The George Hotel, Hathersage
- Rev. Clive Thrower, Ashford in the Water
- Jill Redford, National Centre for English Cultural Tradition

- Leon Russell
- Pickard Communication
- The Sheffield Star
- Catherine Parker
- Nicola Hale
- Chris Broome
- Ben Hale
- Edward Baker

And many other people I have met with or spoken to whilst doing this book. Their help and enthusiasm was most appreciated

*What life is this if,
full of care, we have
no time to stop
and stare...*